EASTER

Coloring Book

EASTER
Coloring Book

Silhouette Leah

Copyright:

Printed in the United States of America

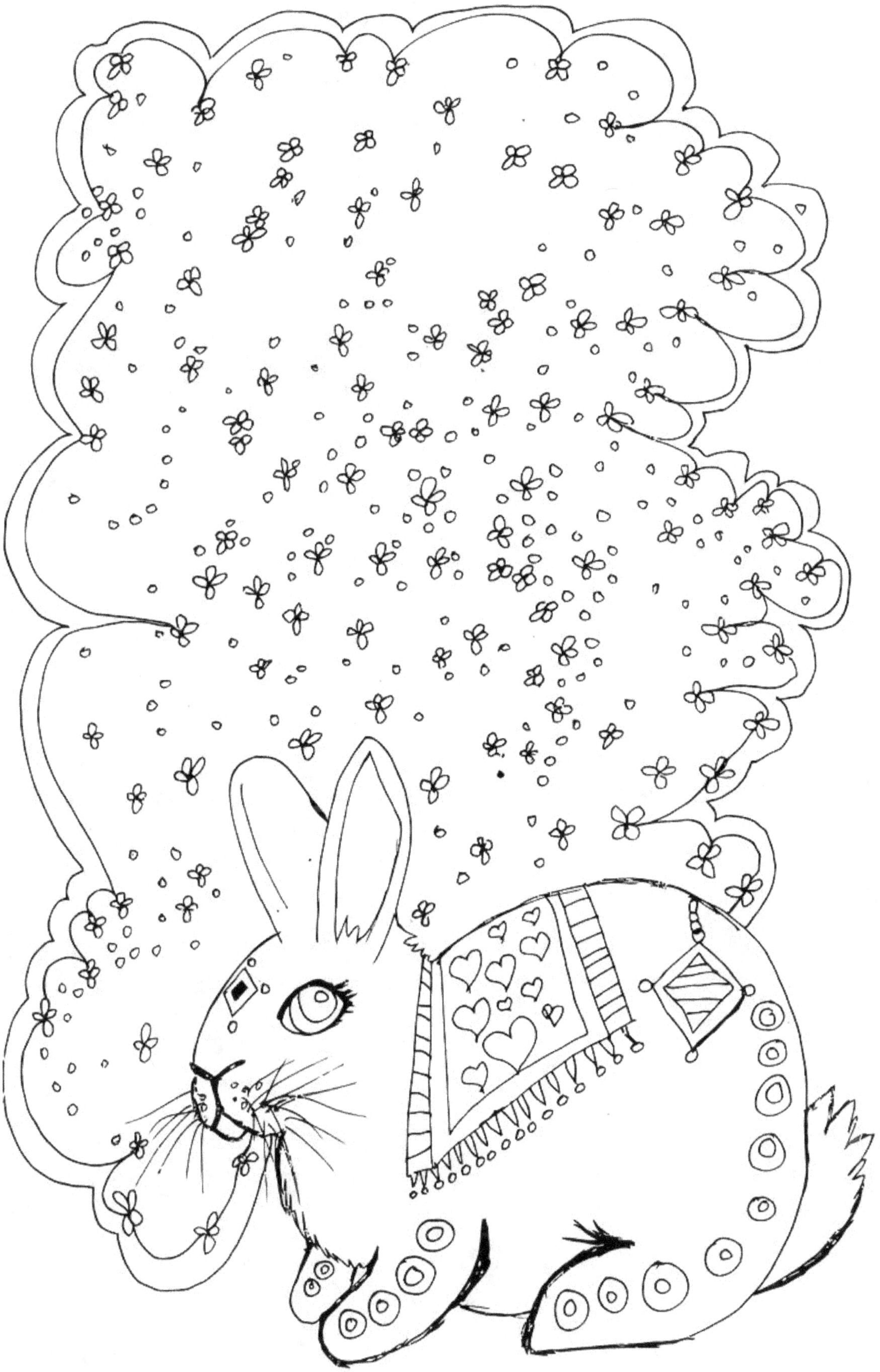

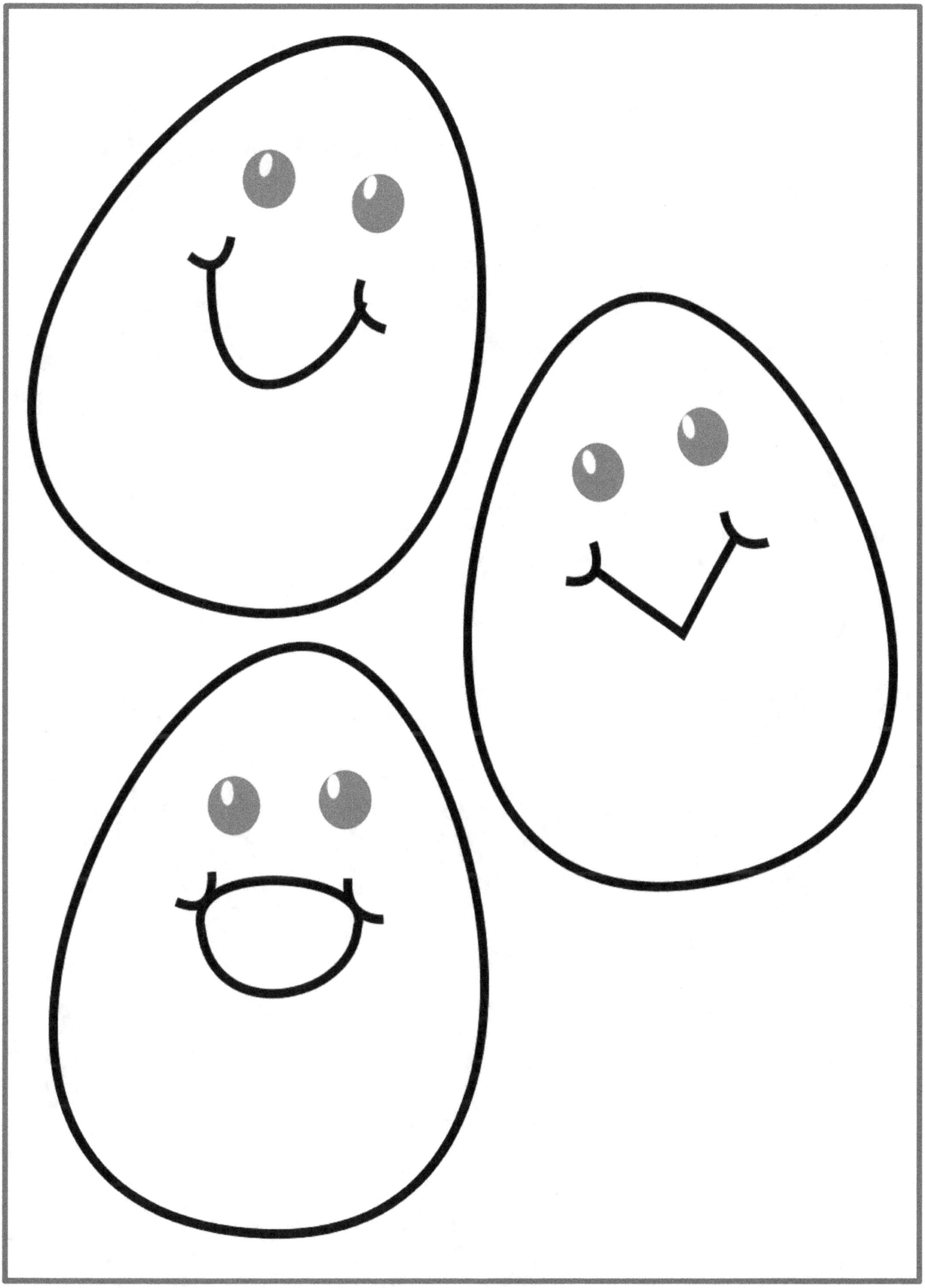

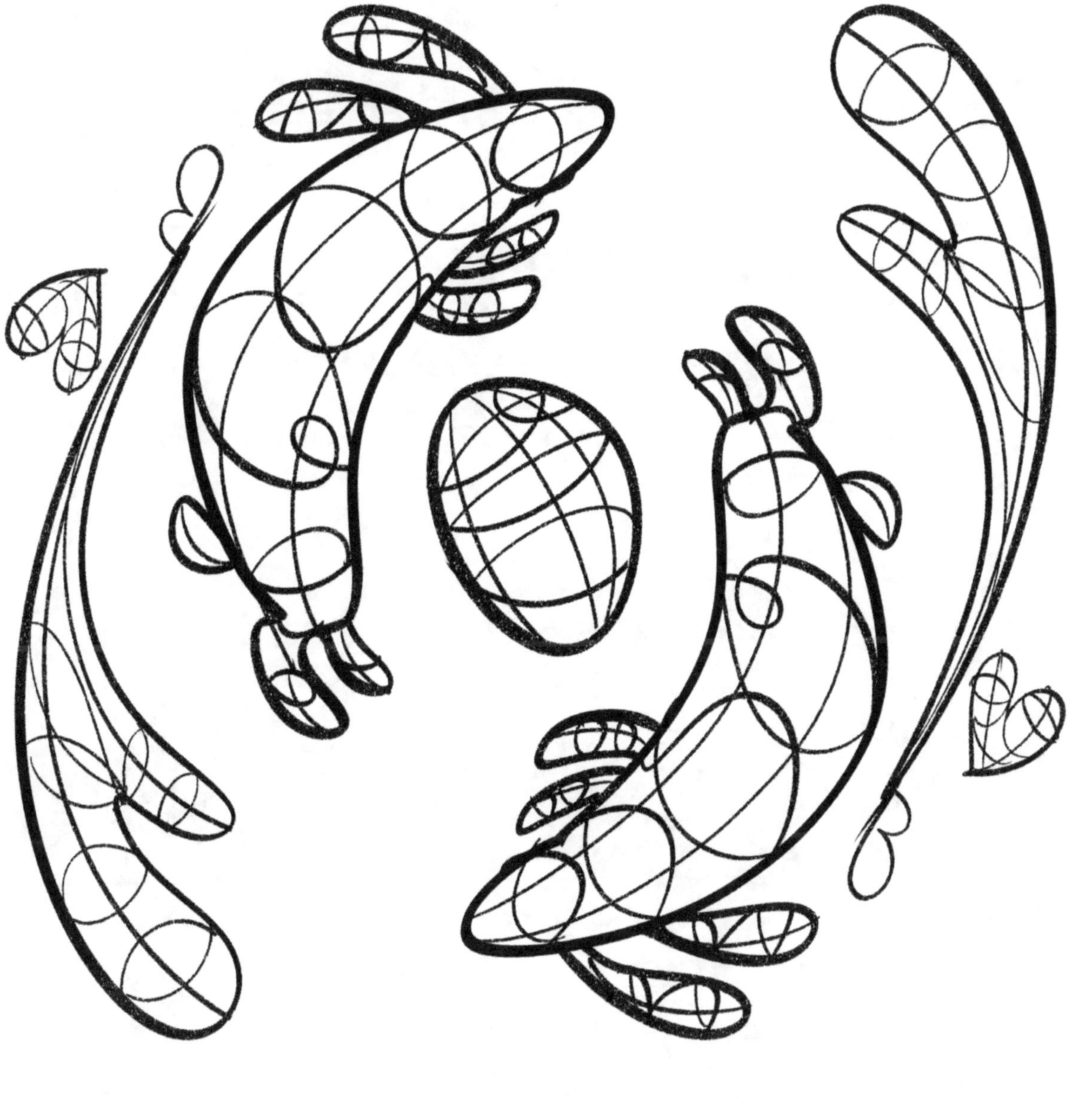

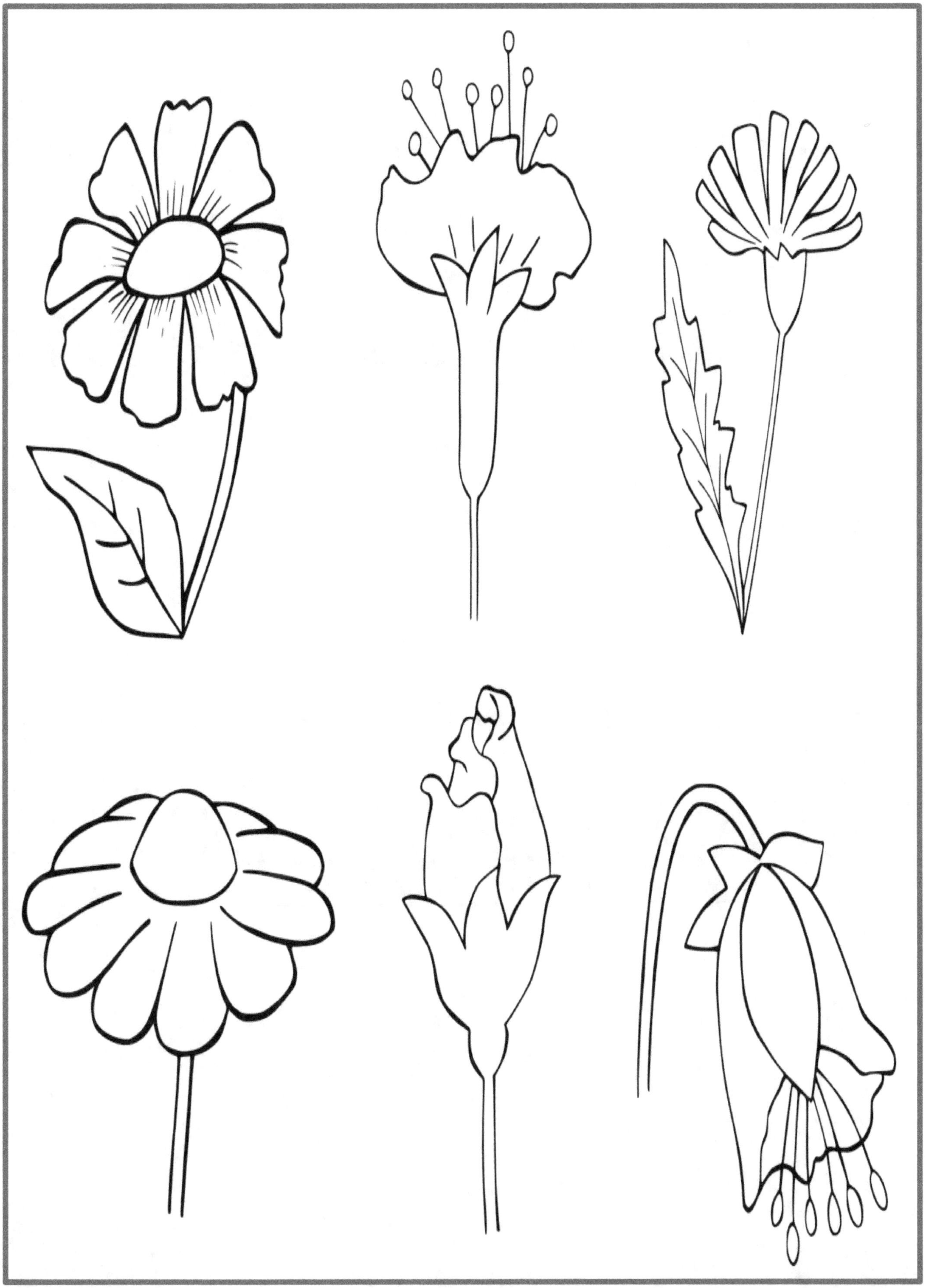

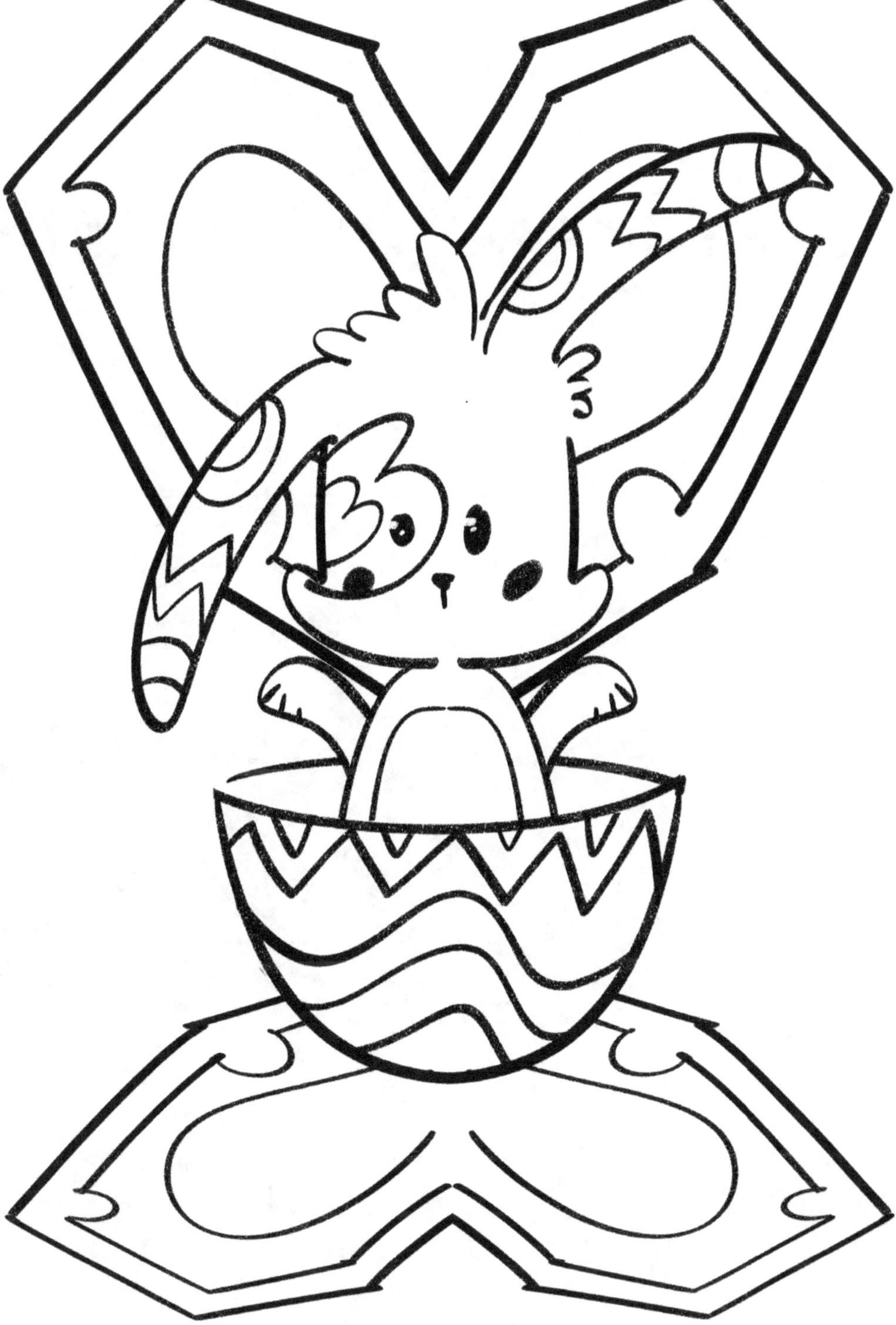

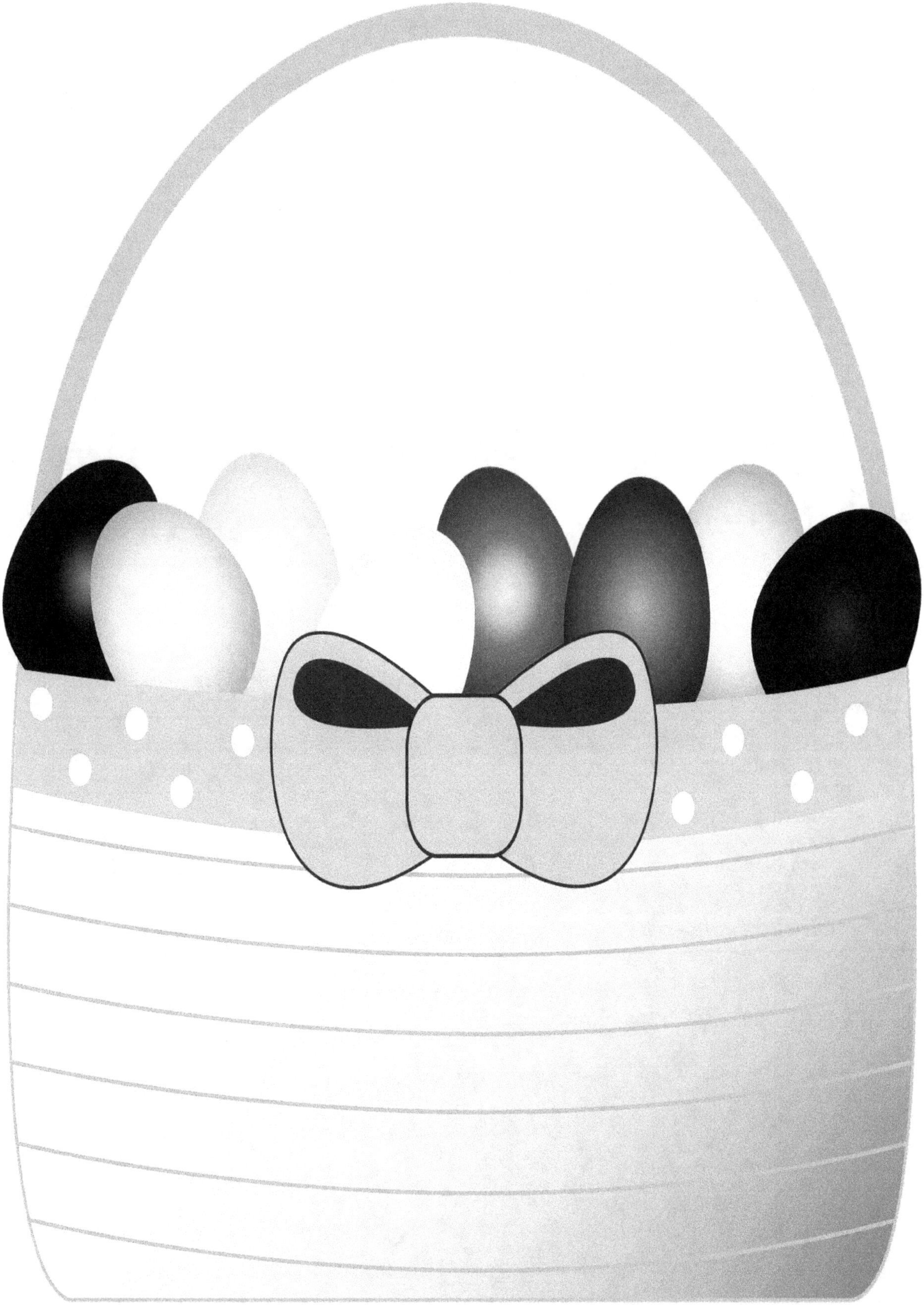

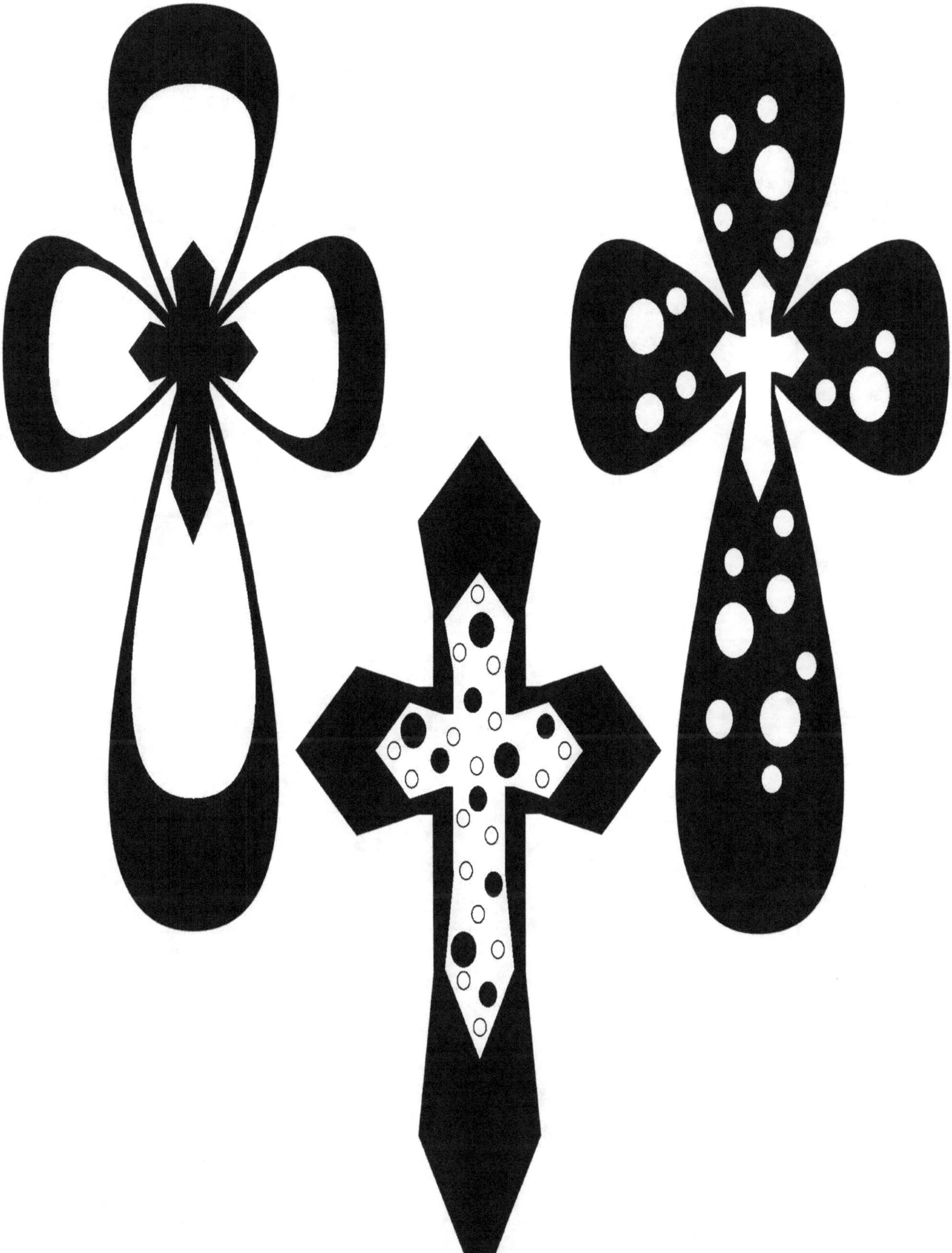

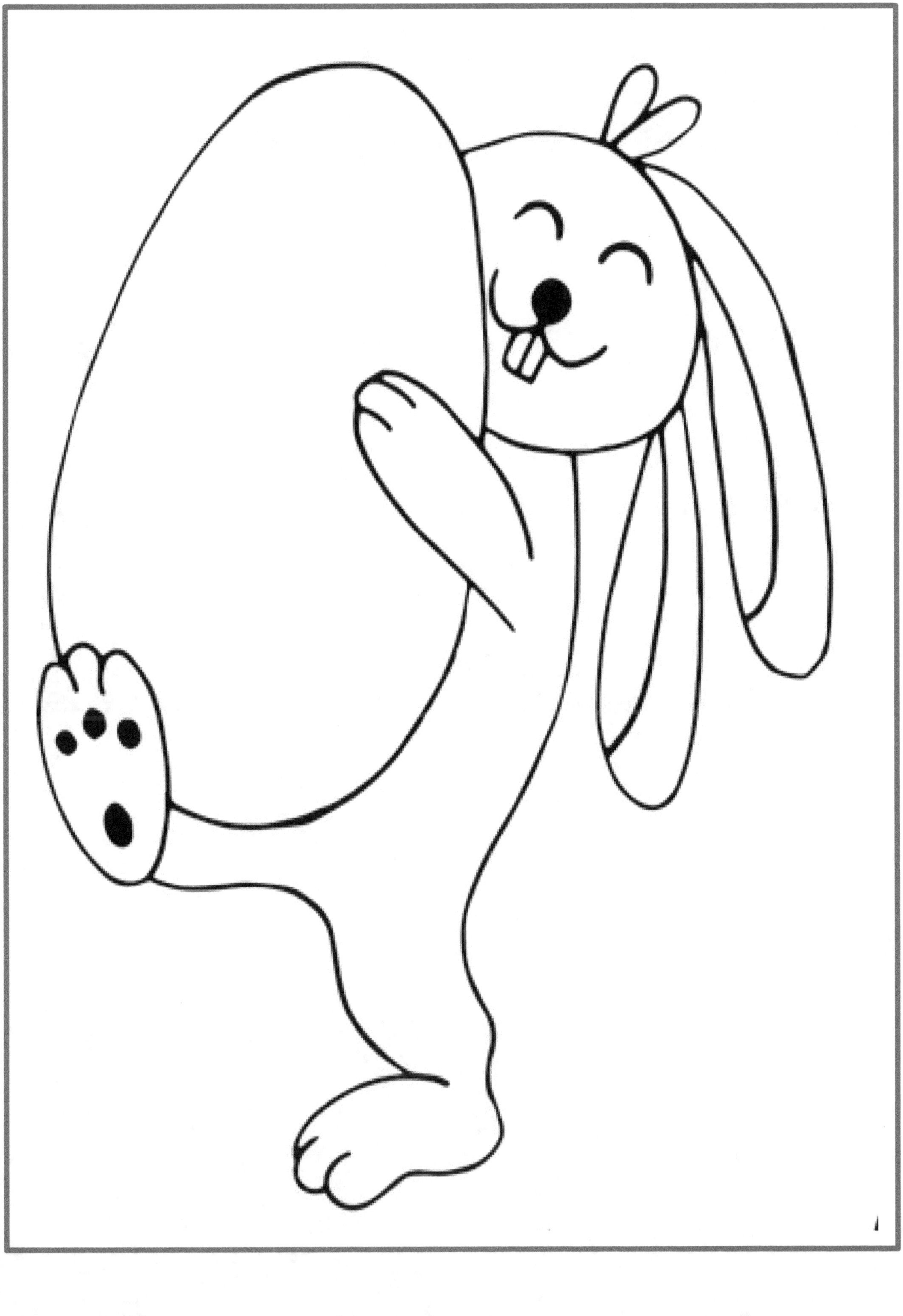

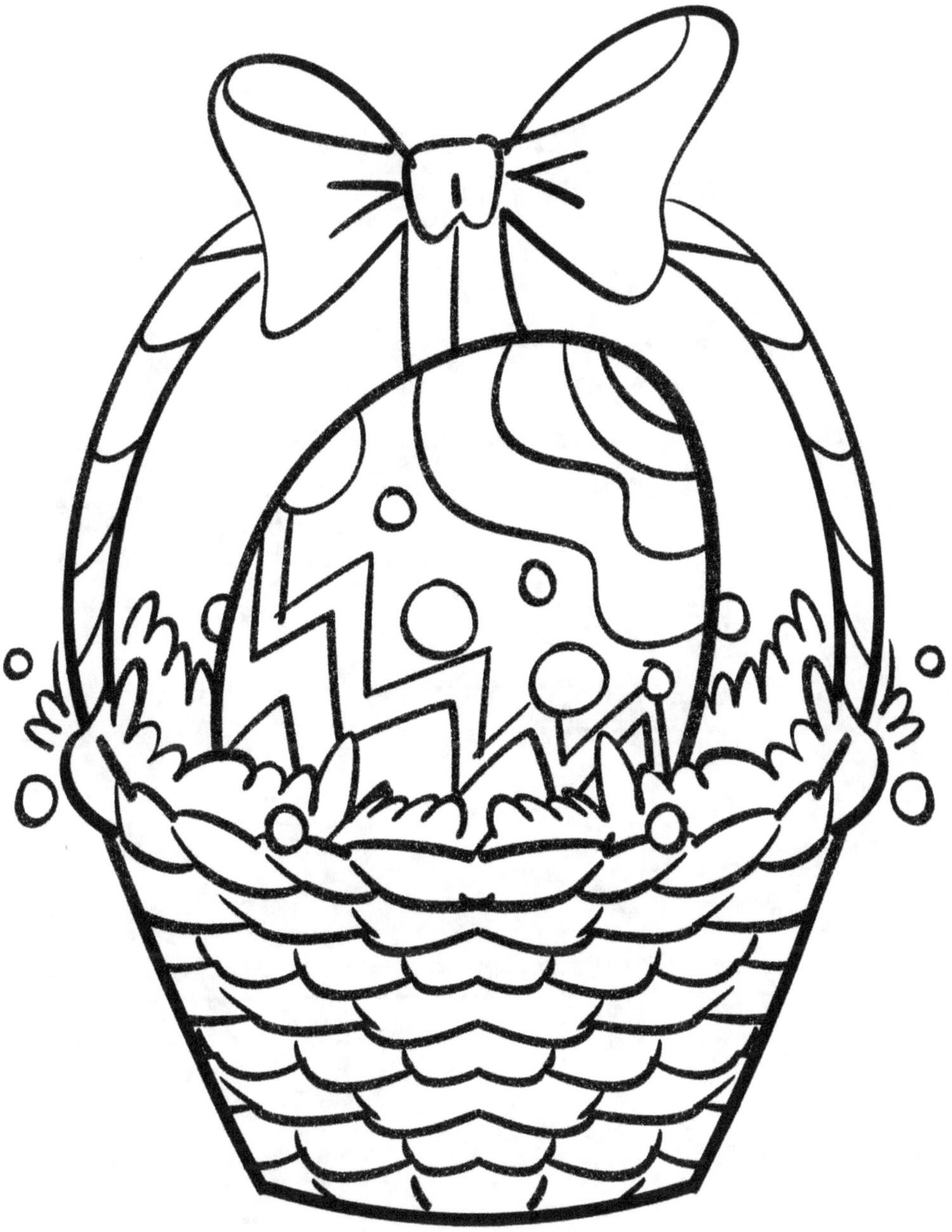

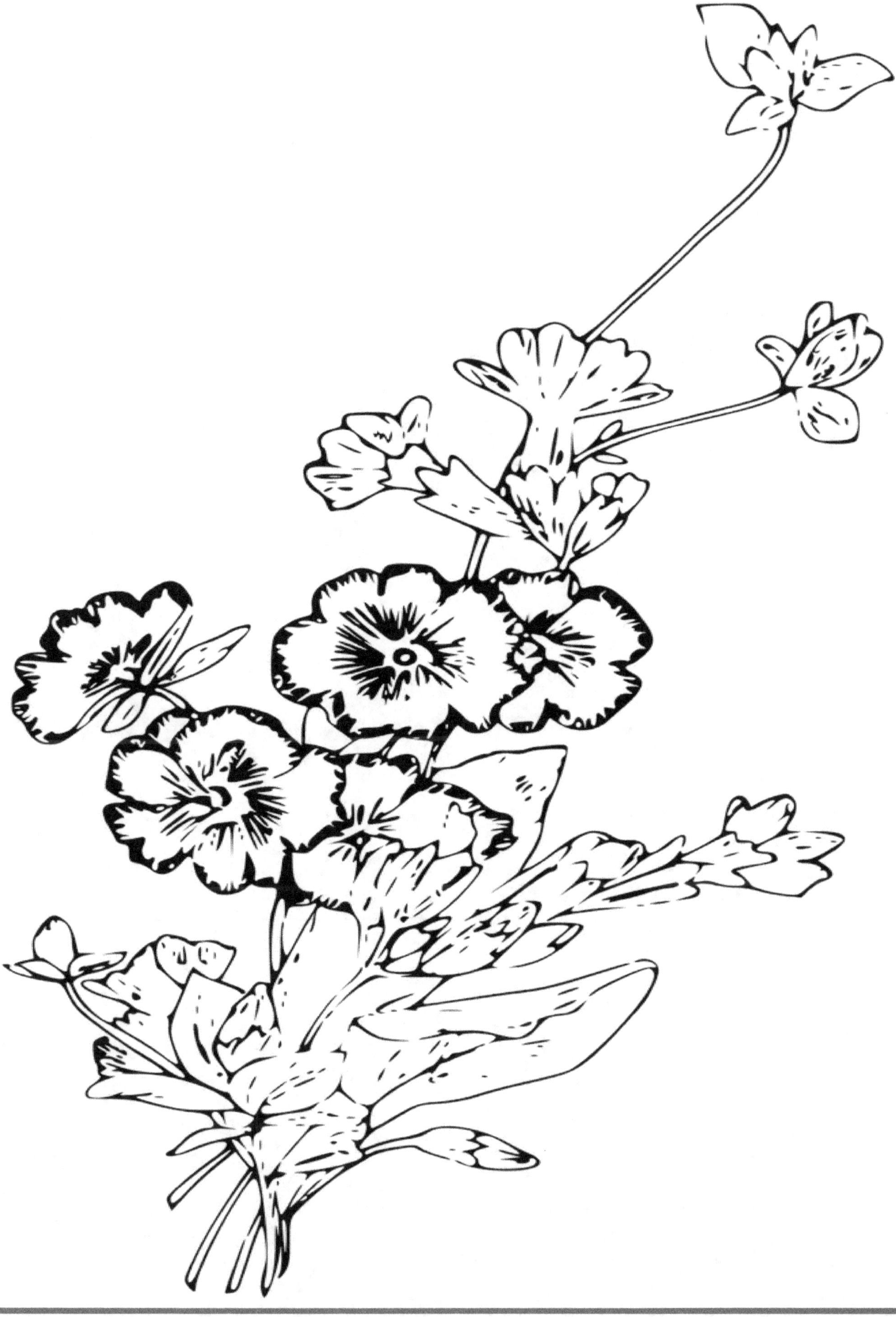

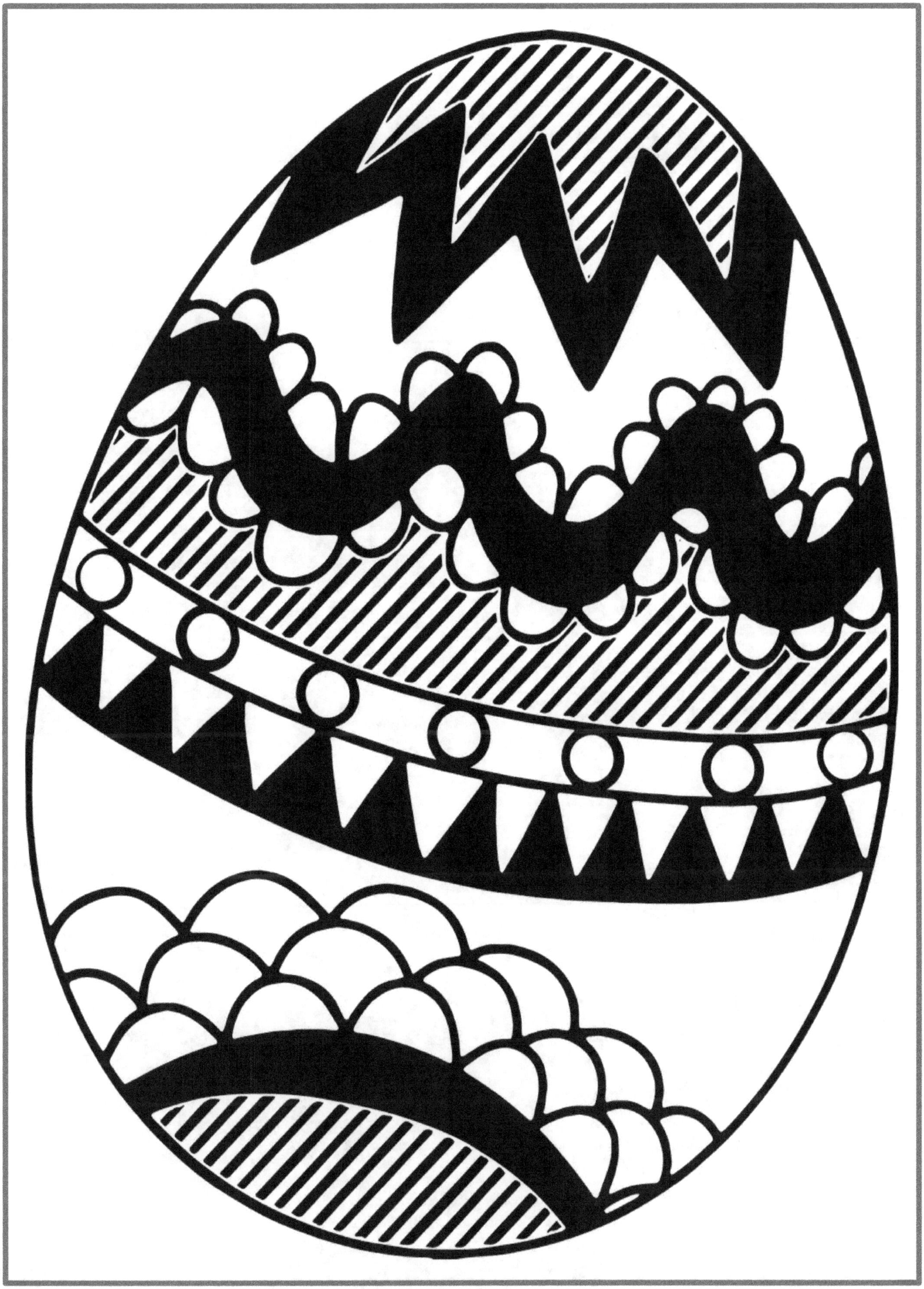

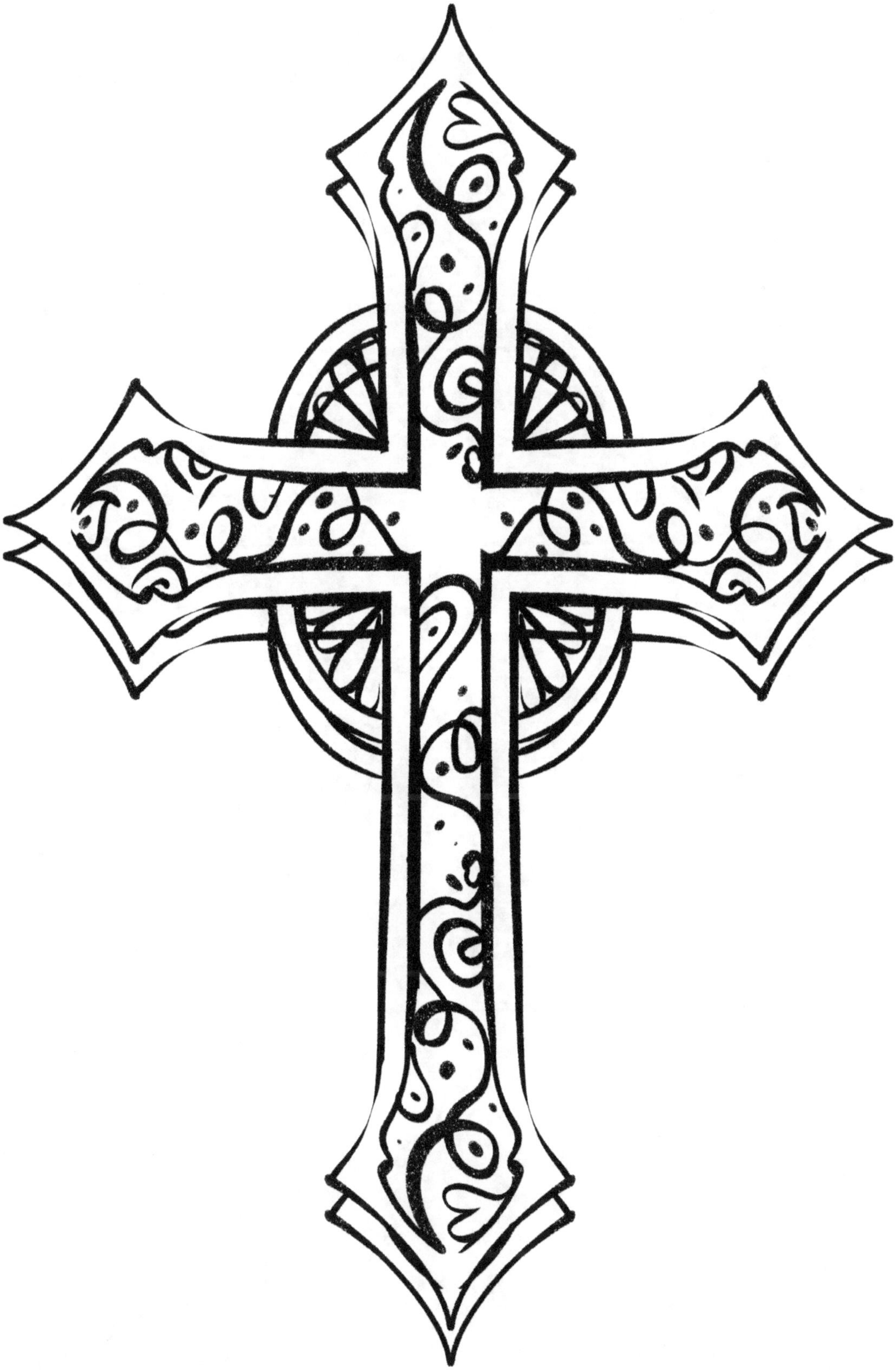

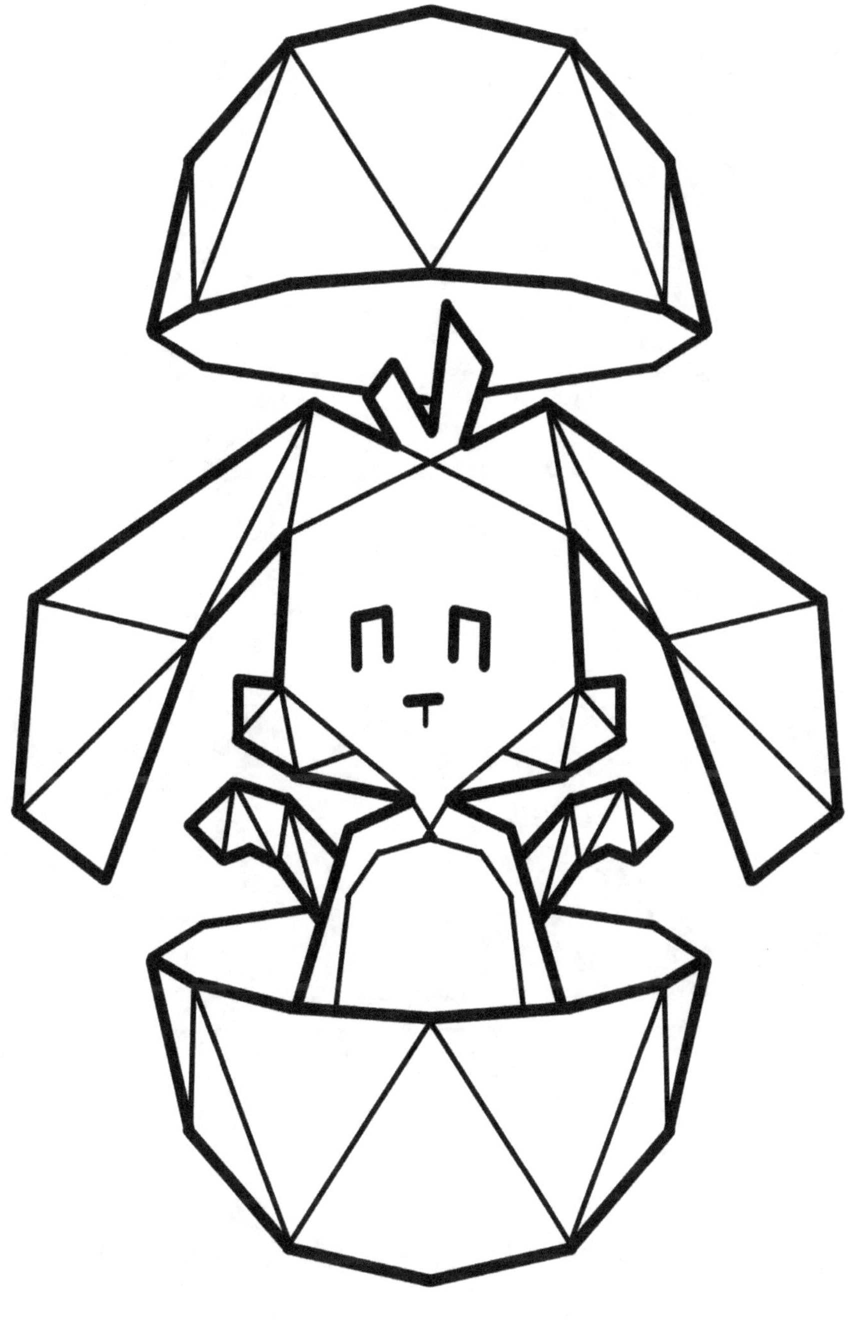

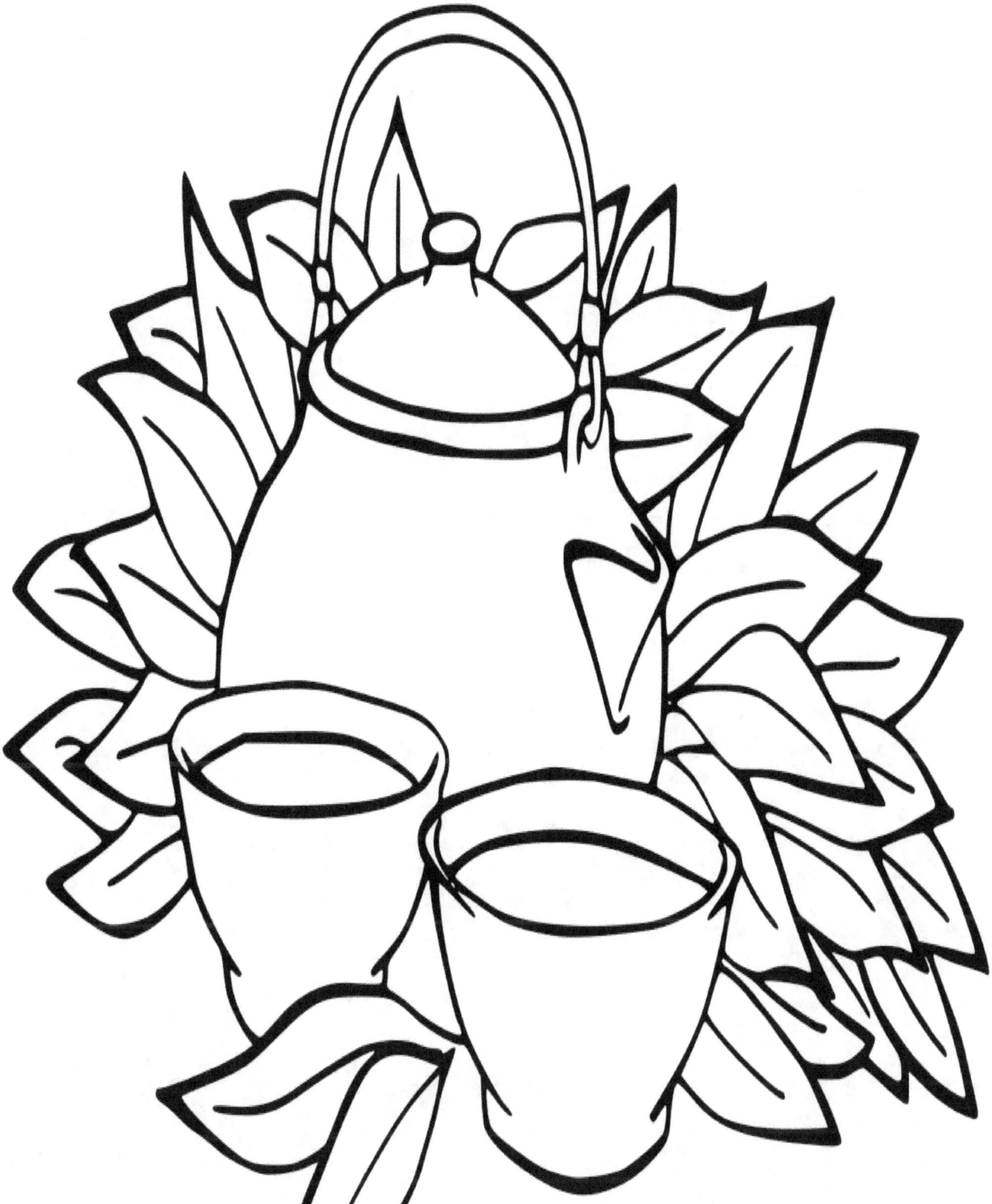

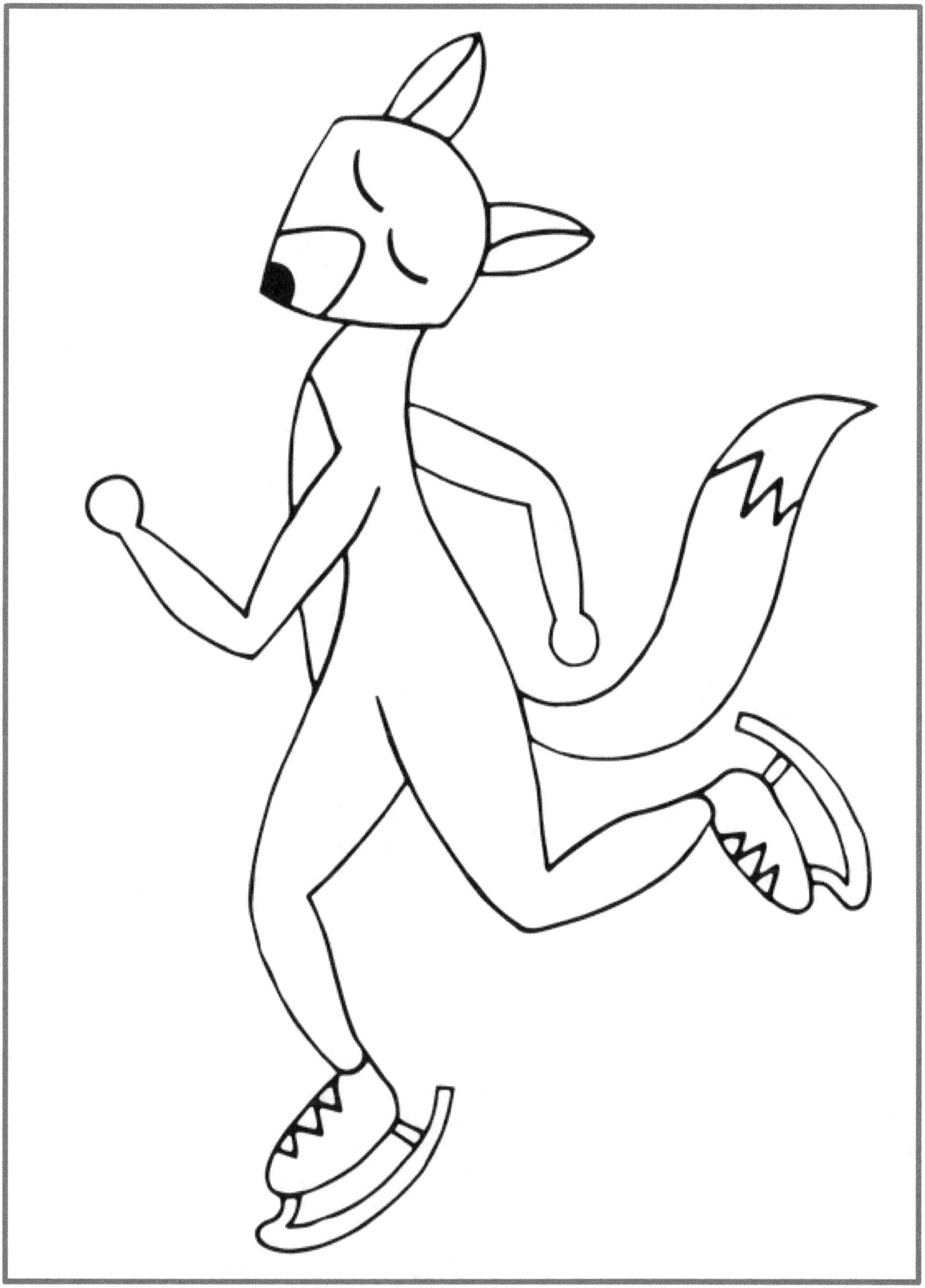

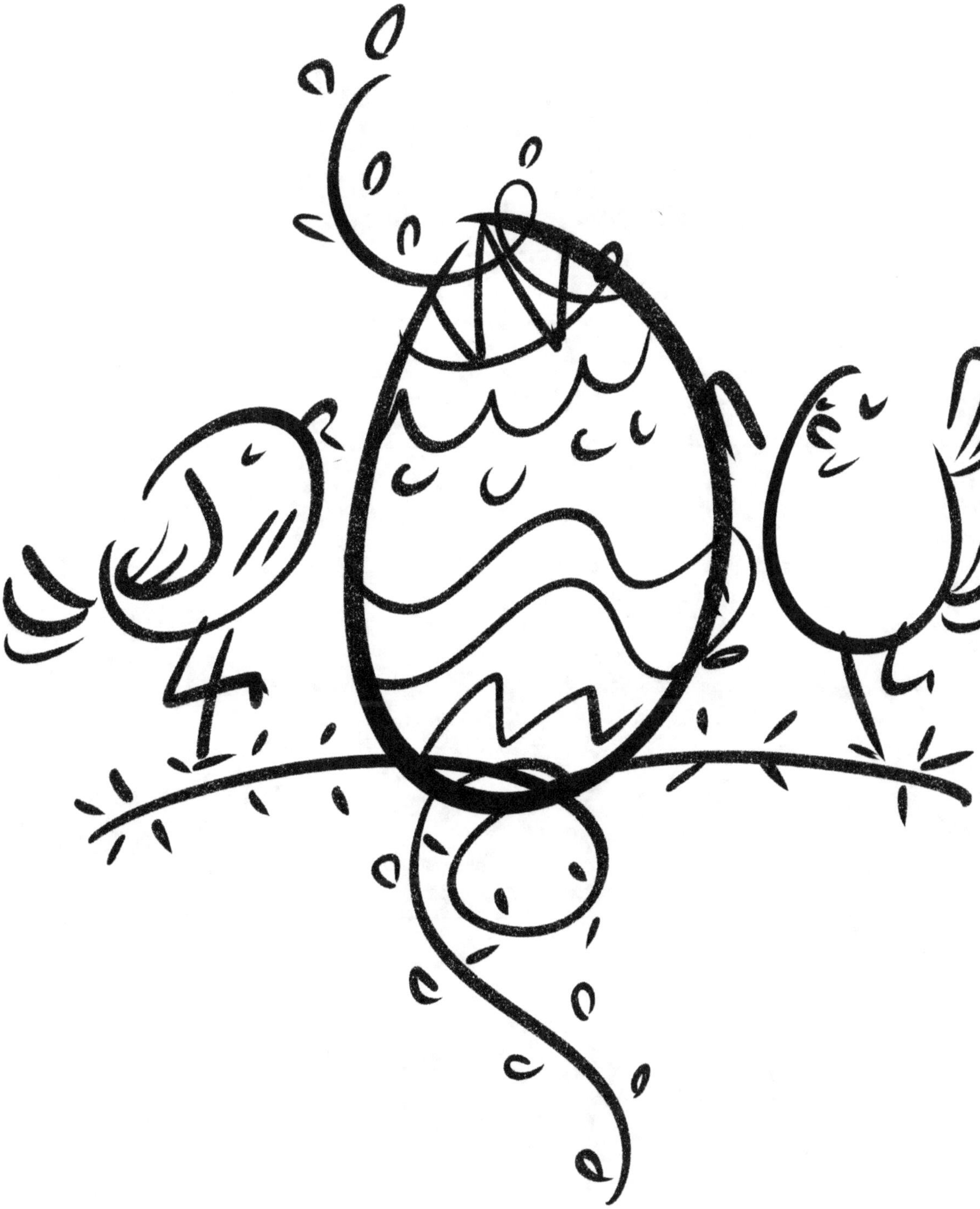

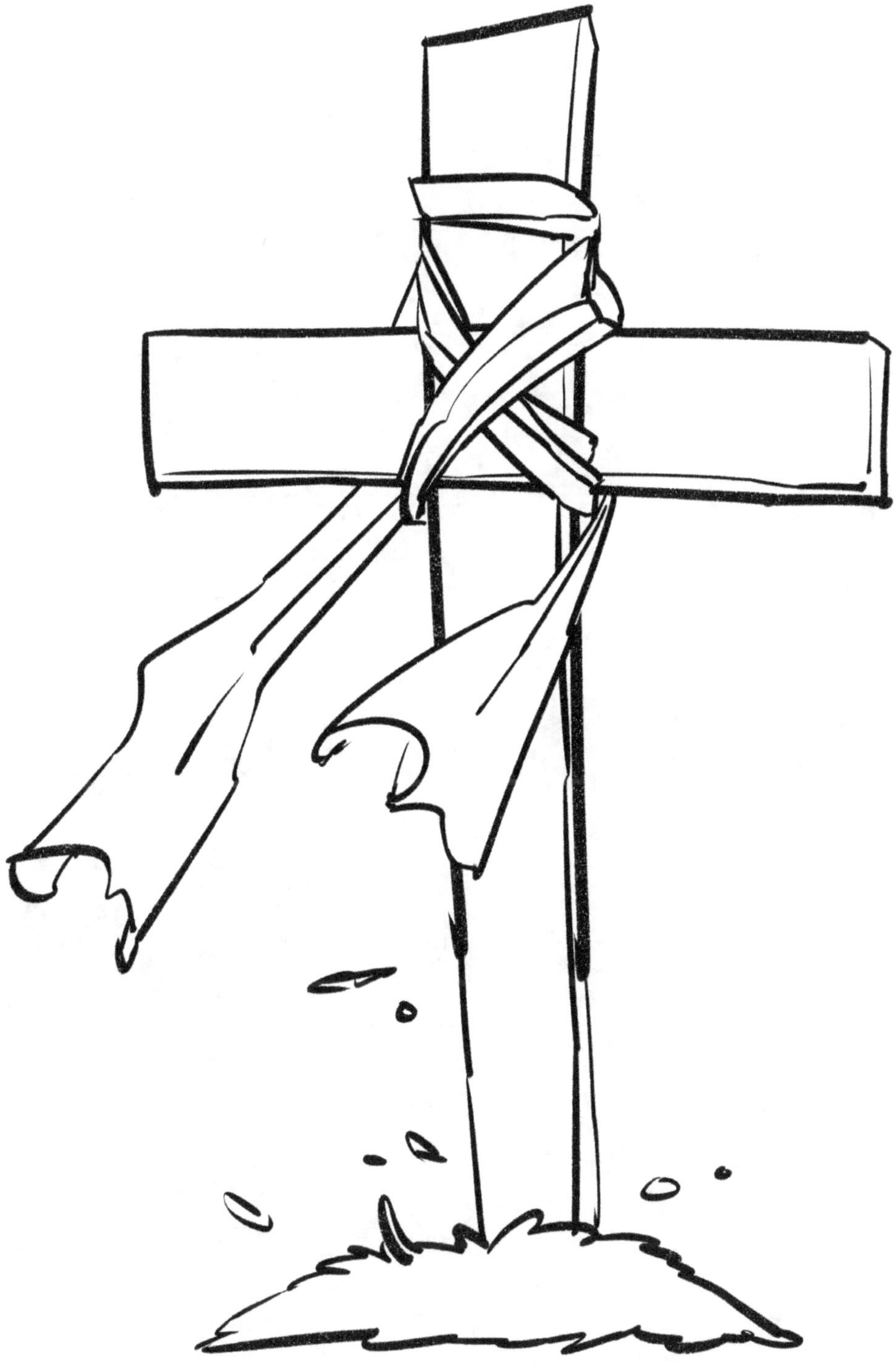

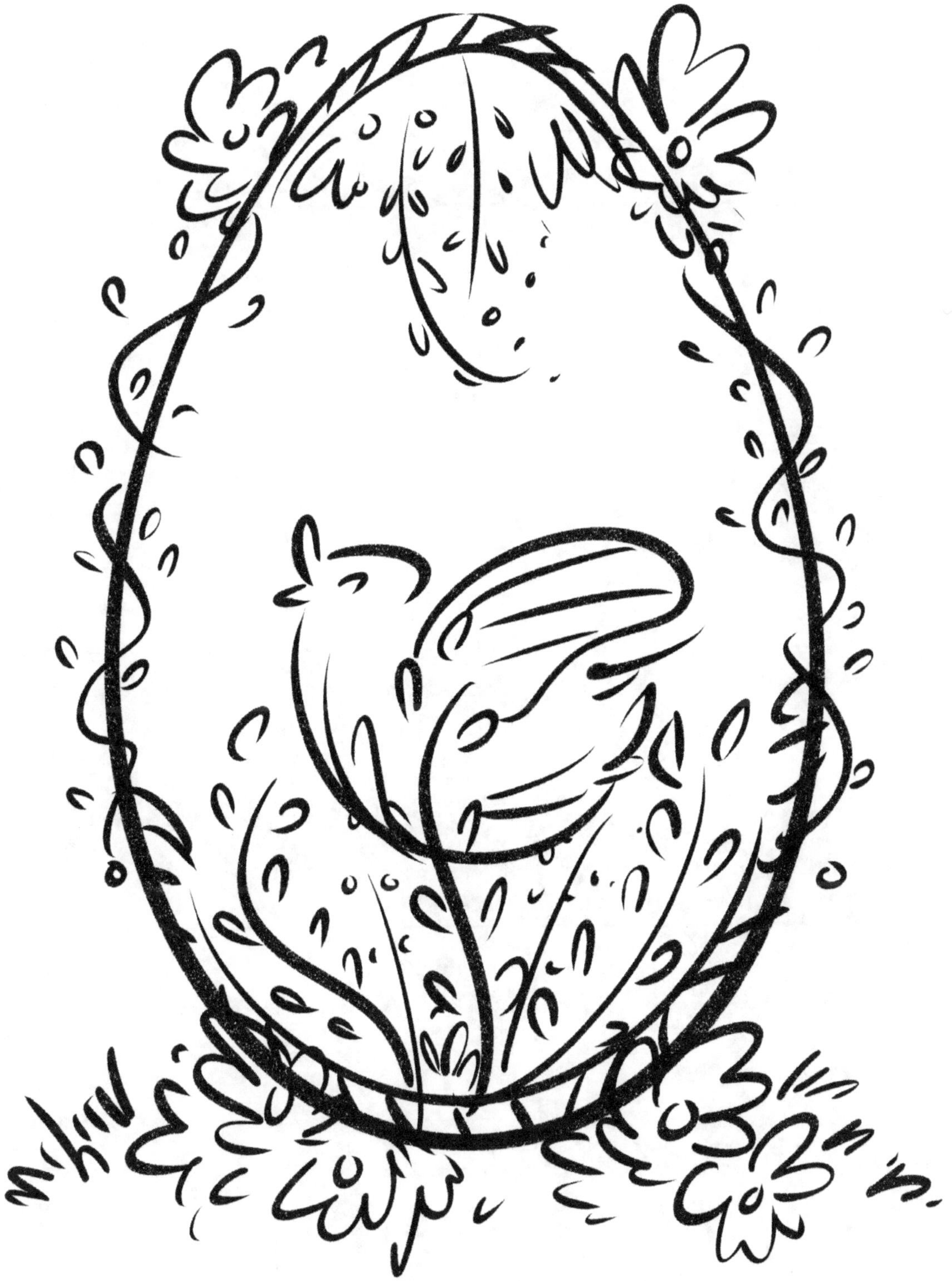

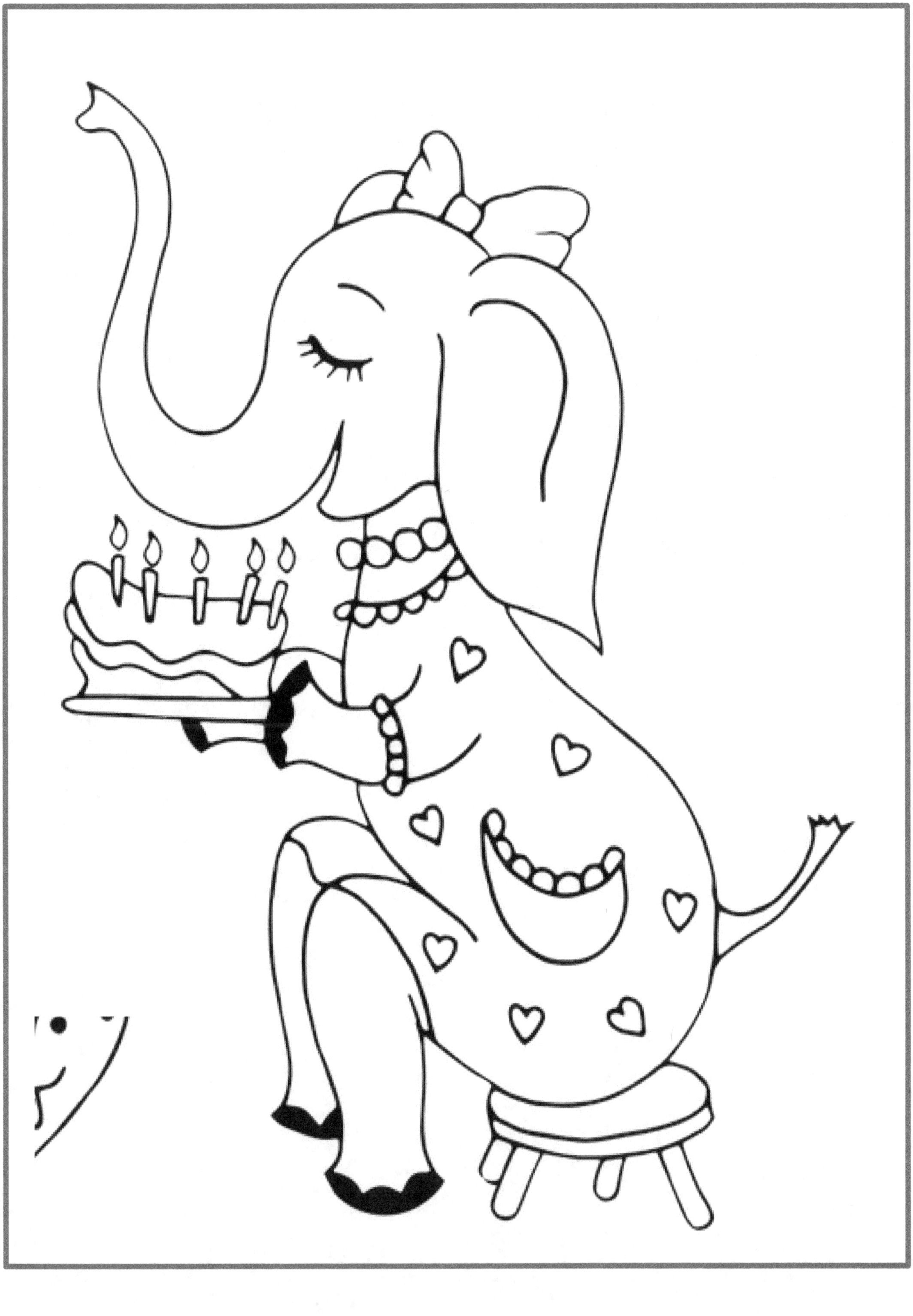

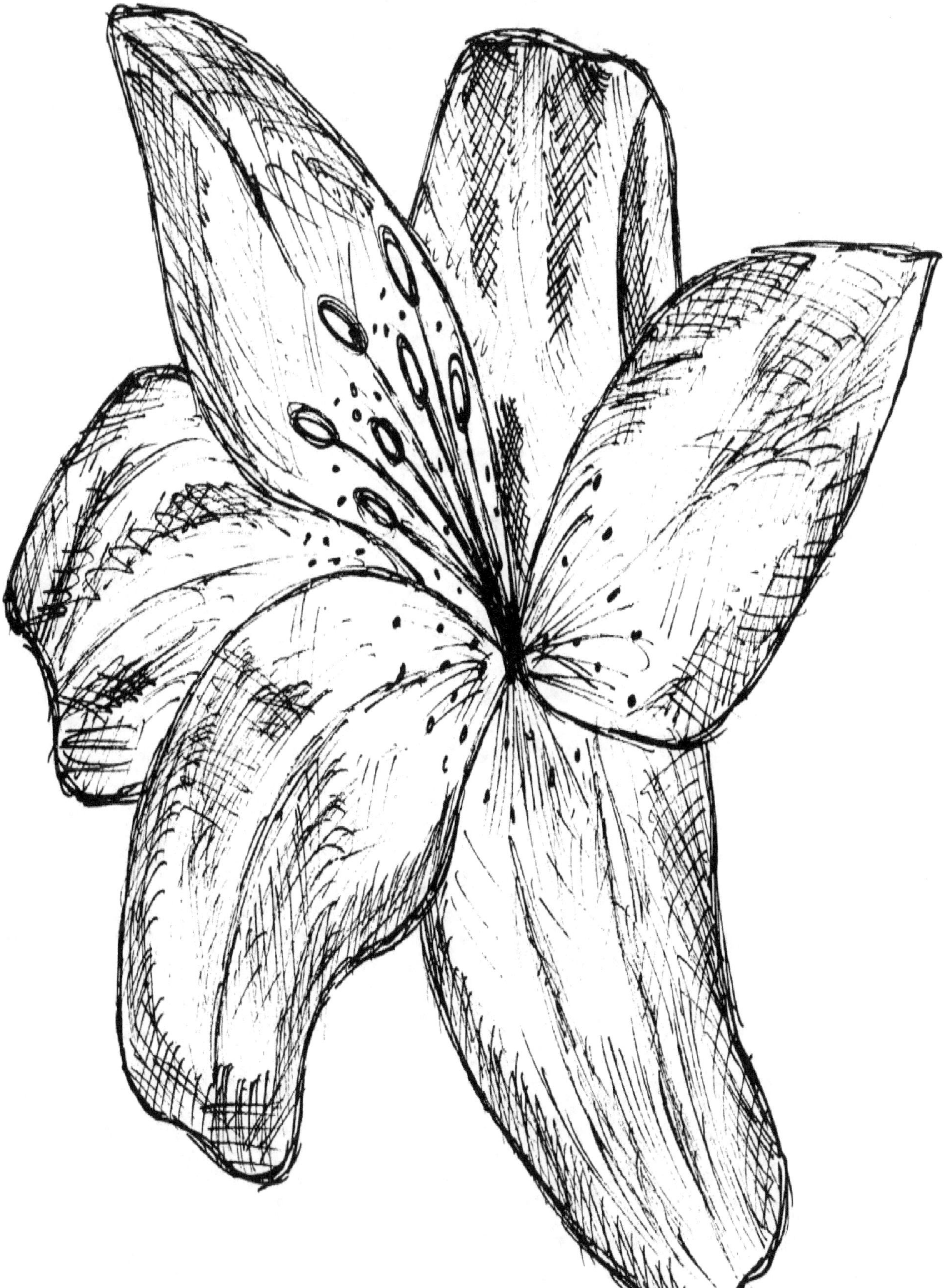

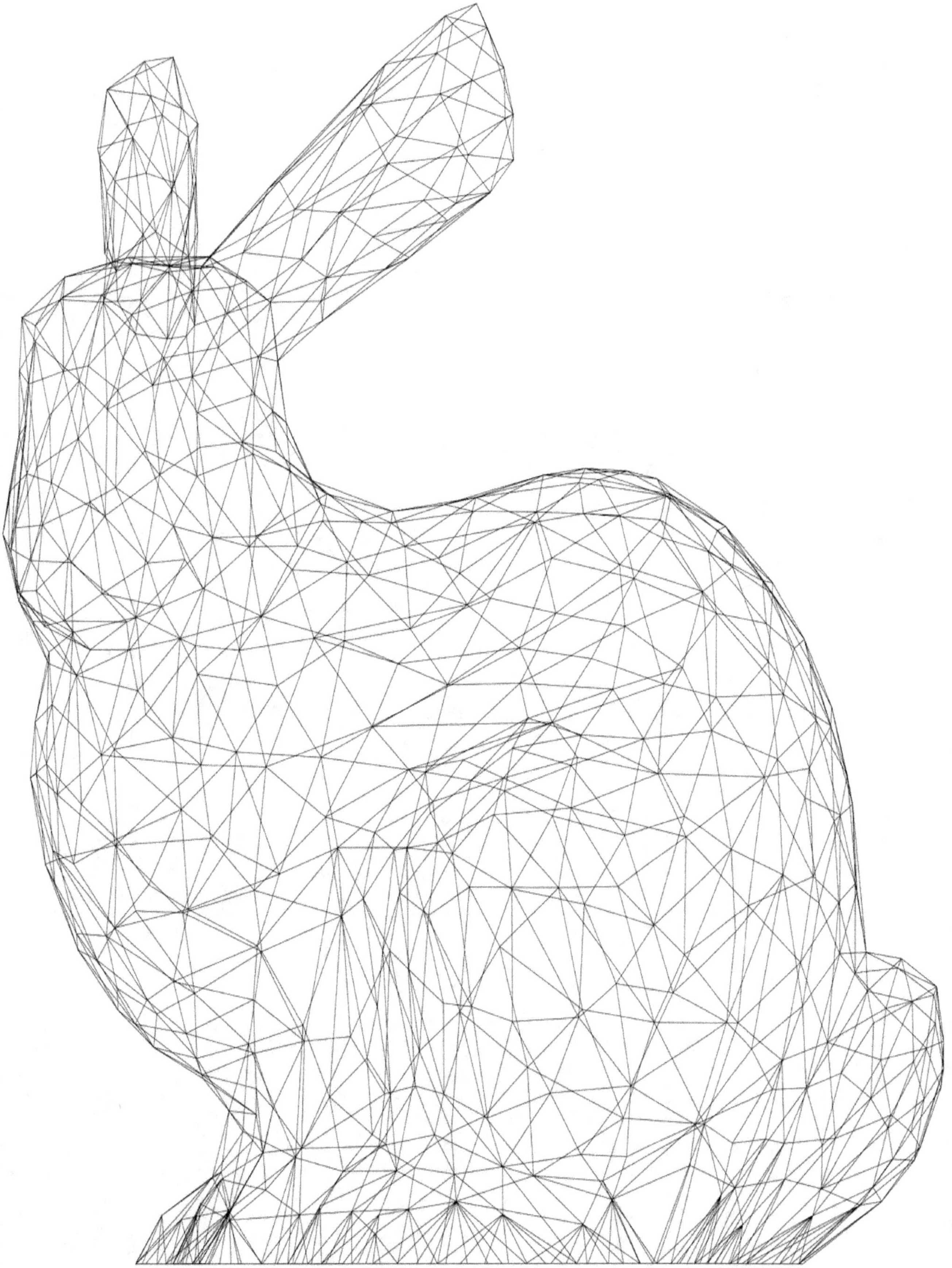

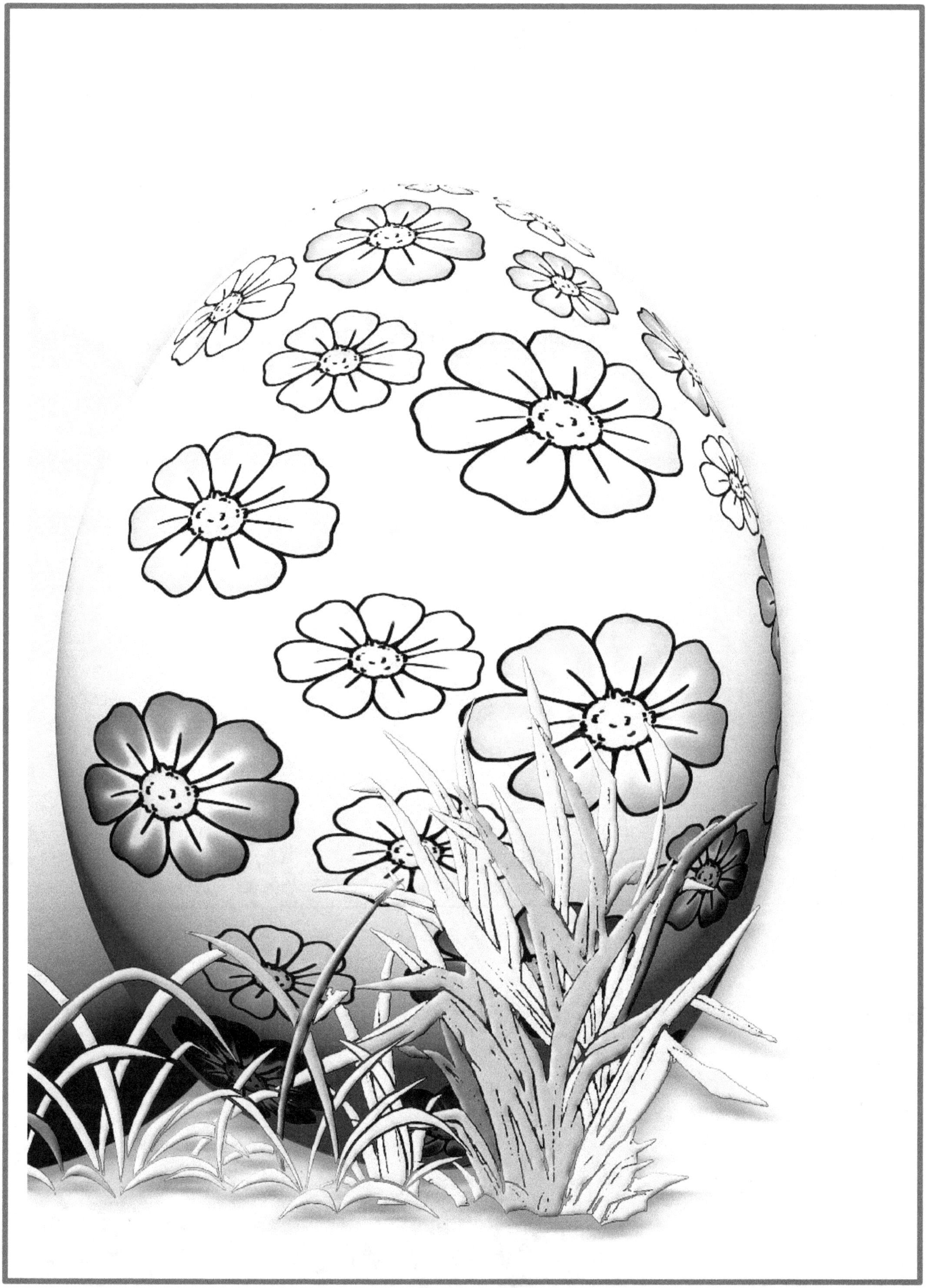

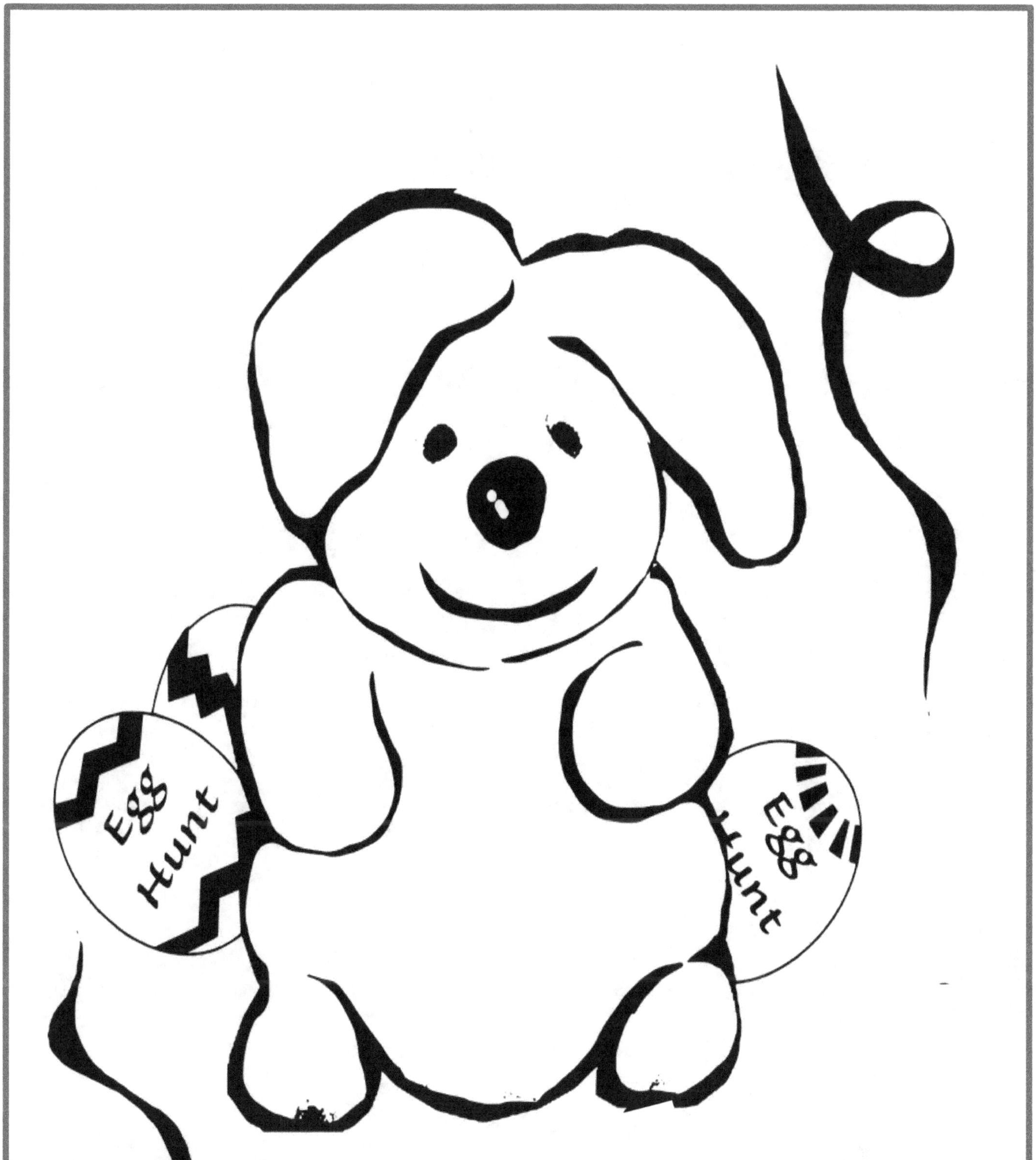
Egg
Hunt
Egg
Hunt

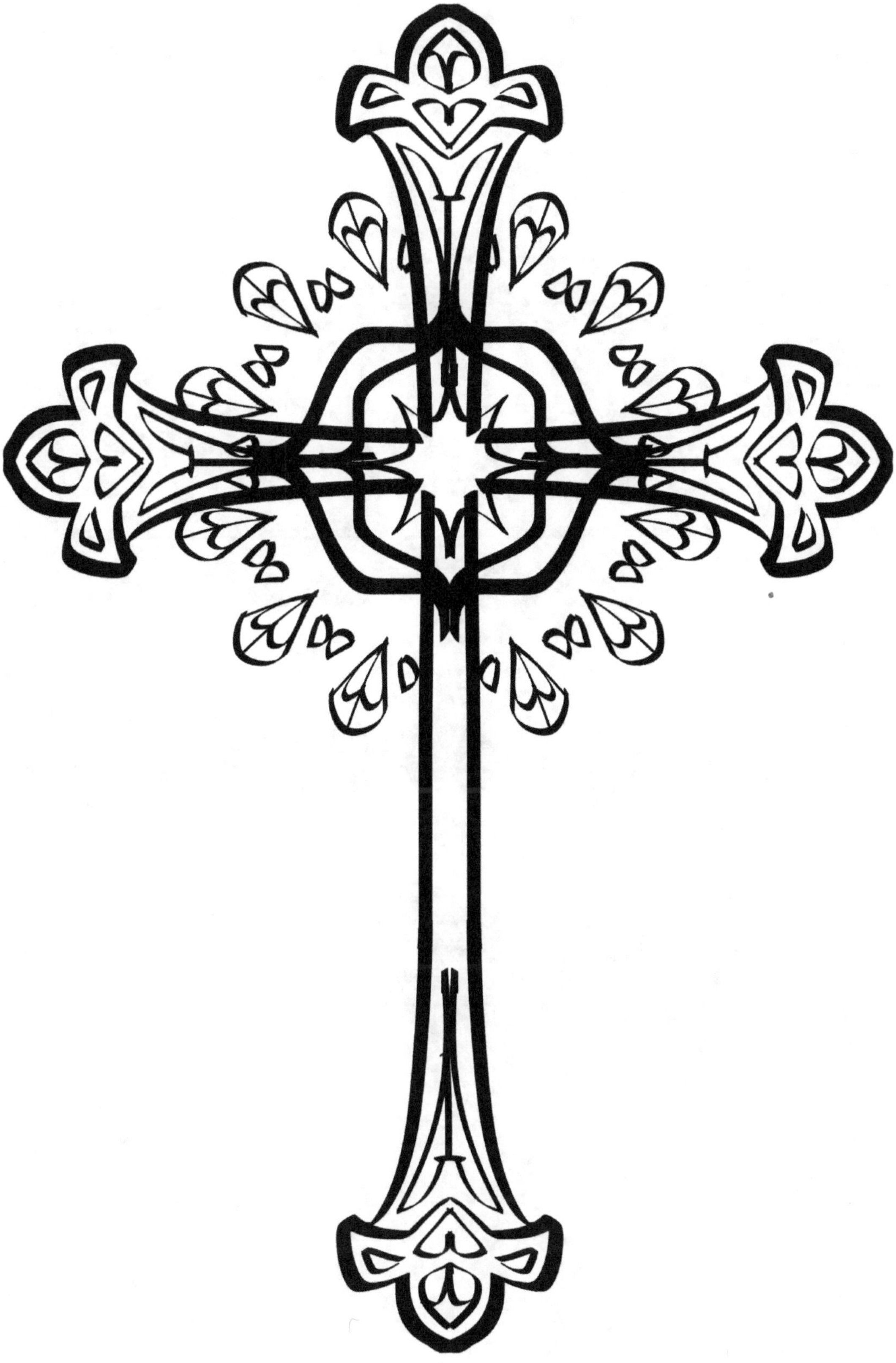

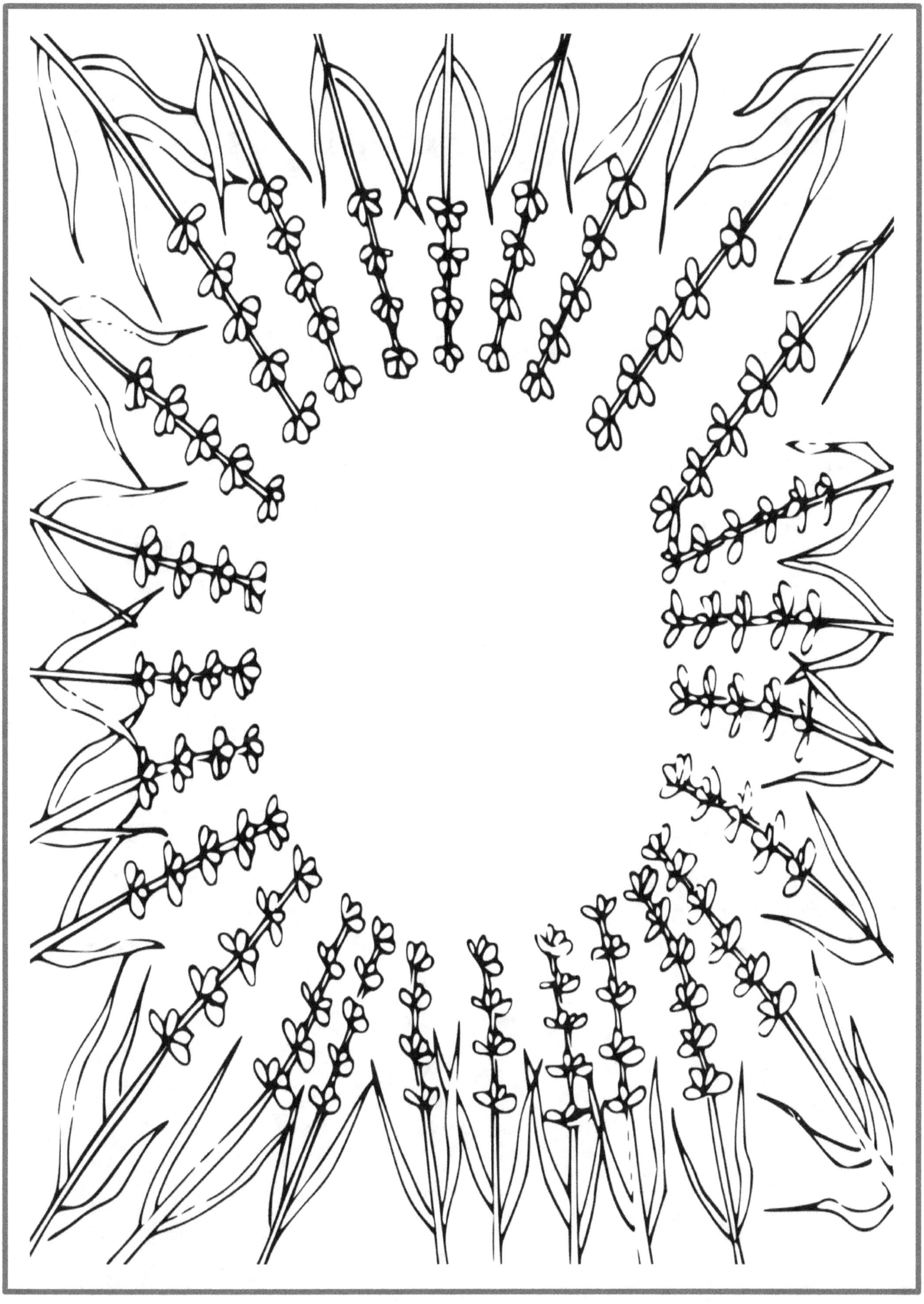

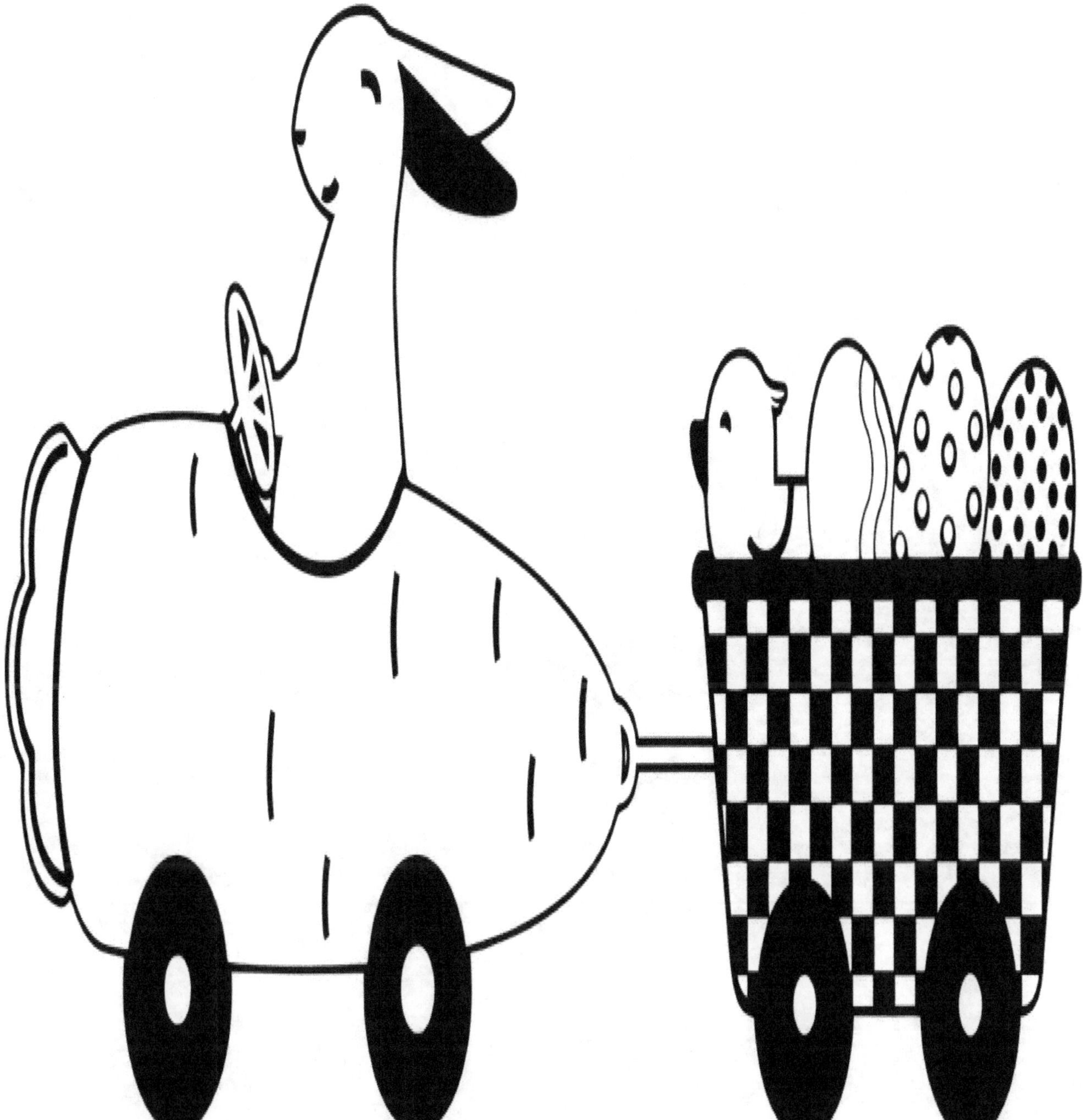

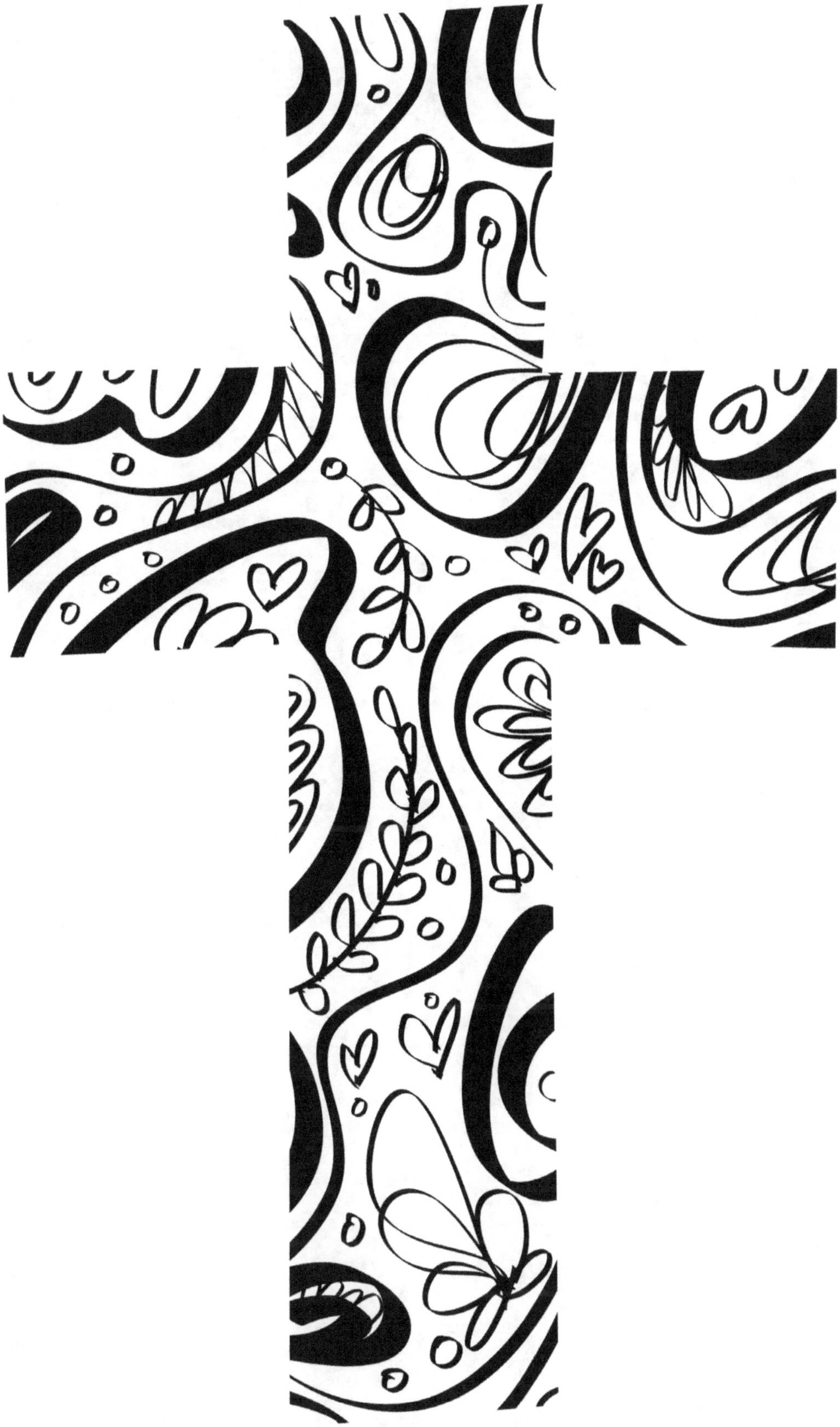

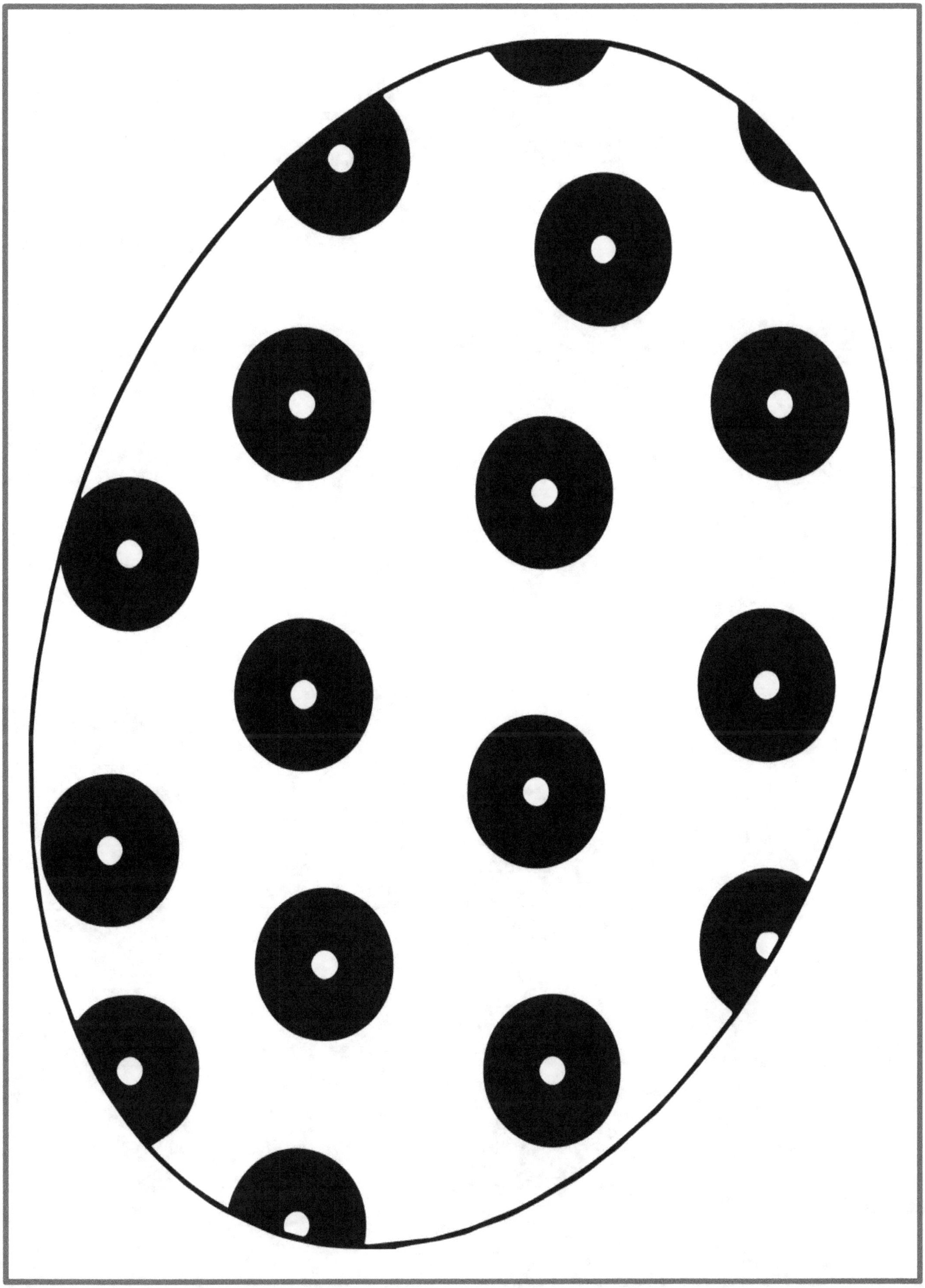

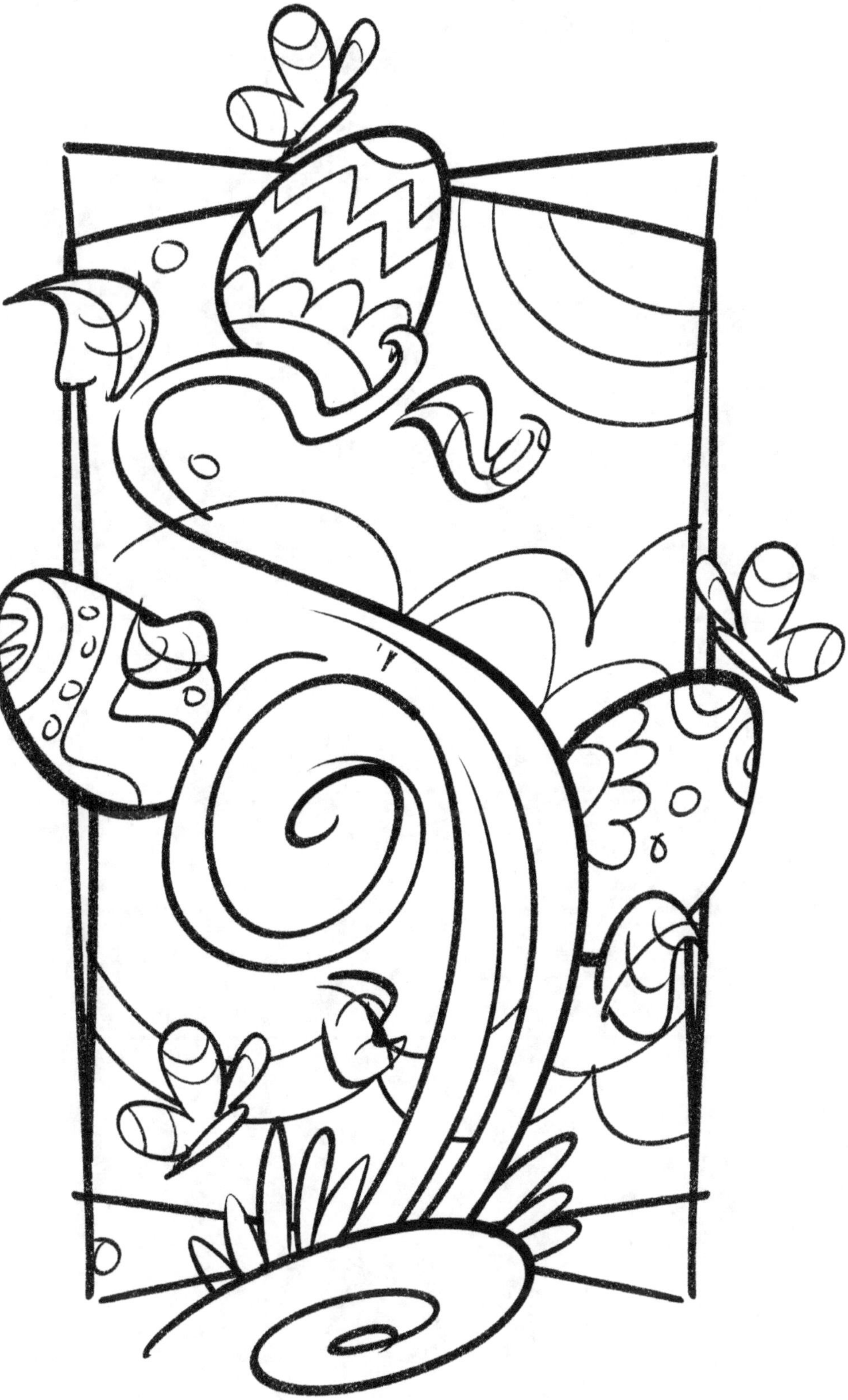

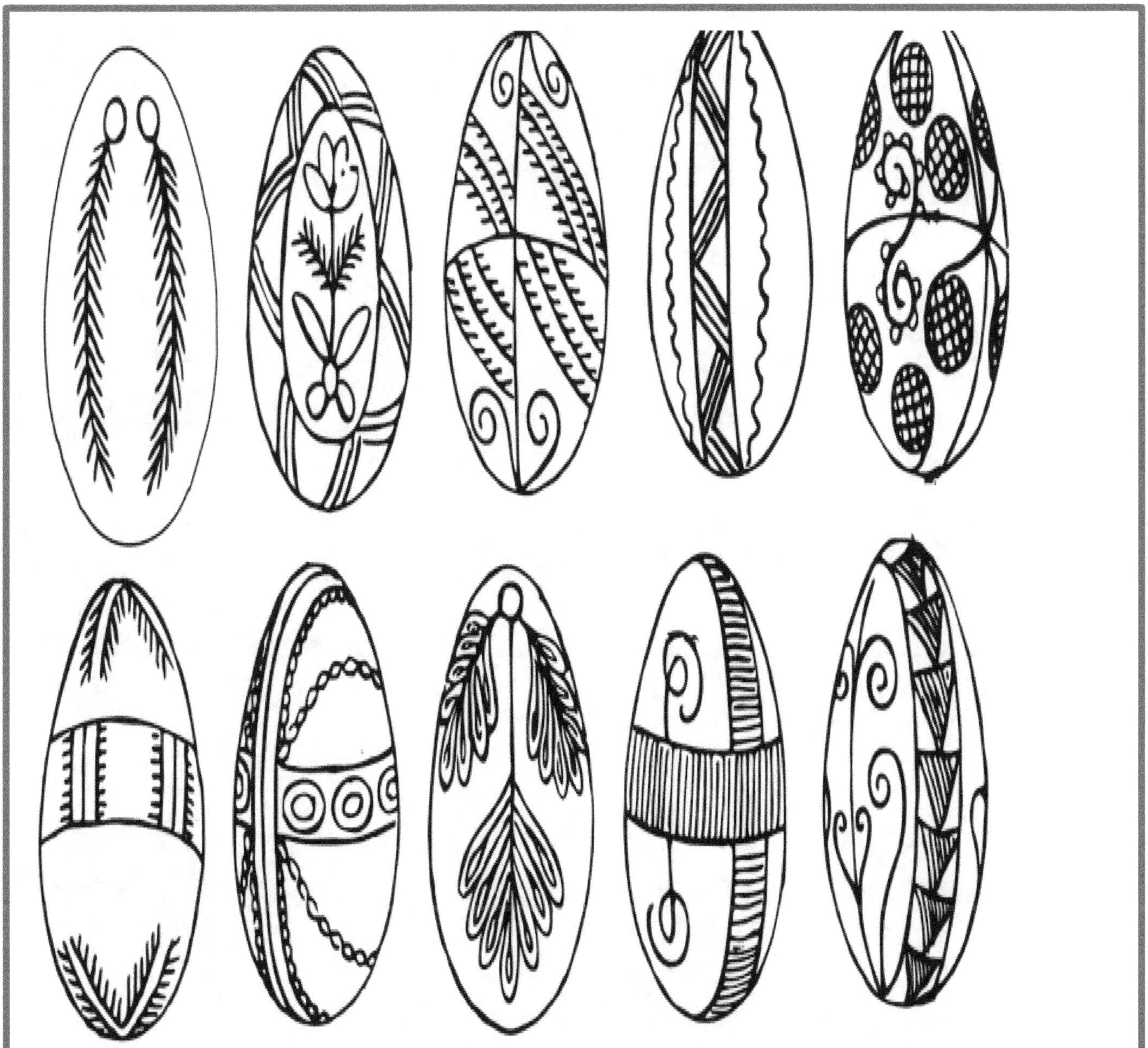

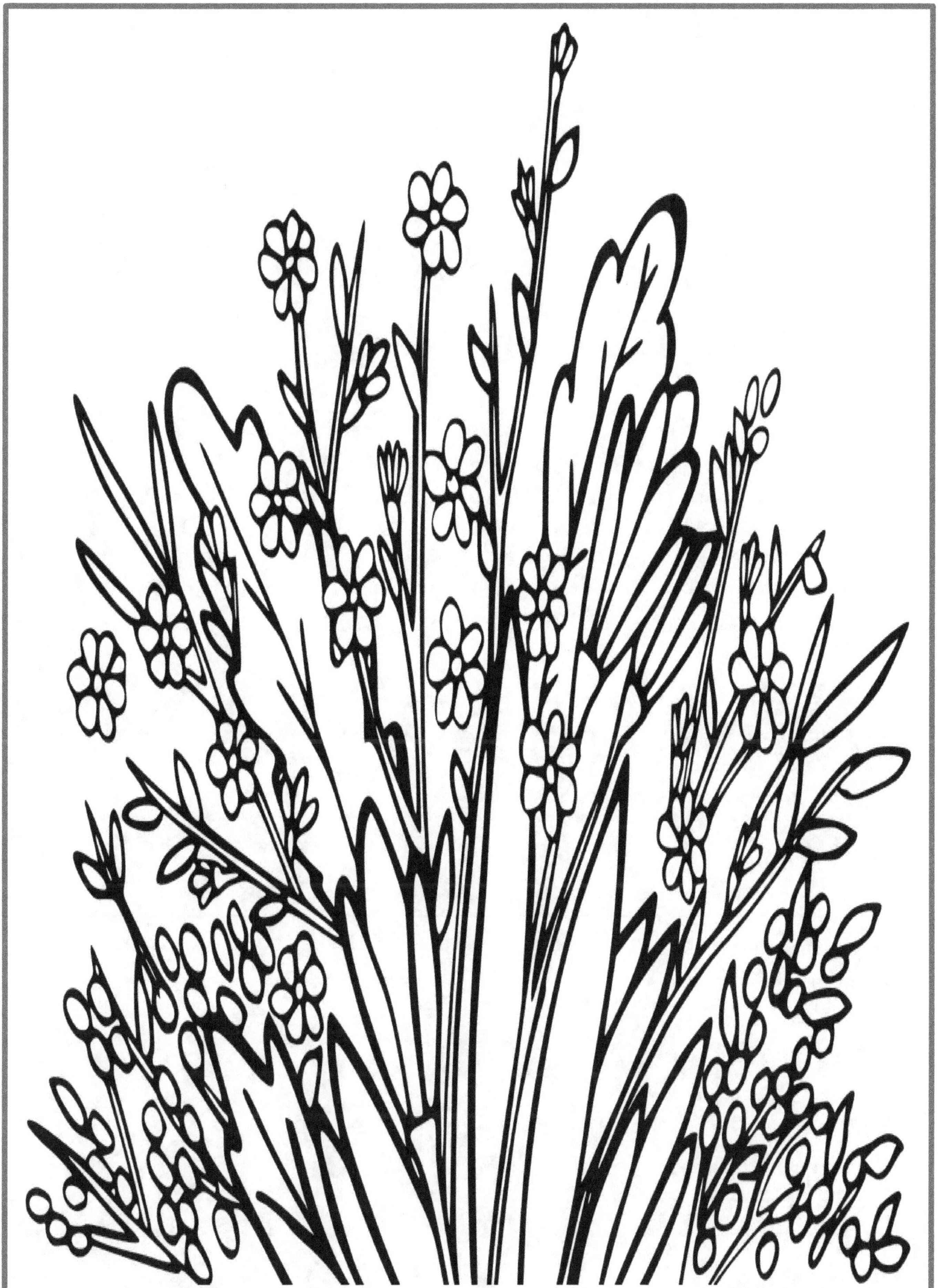

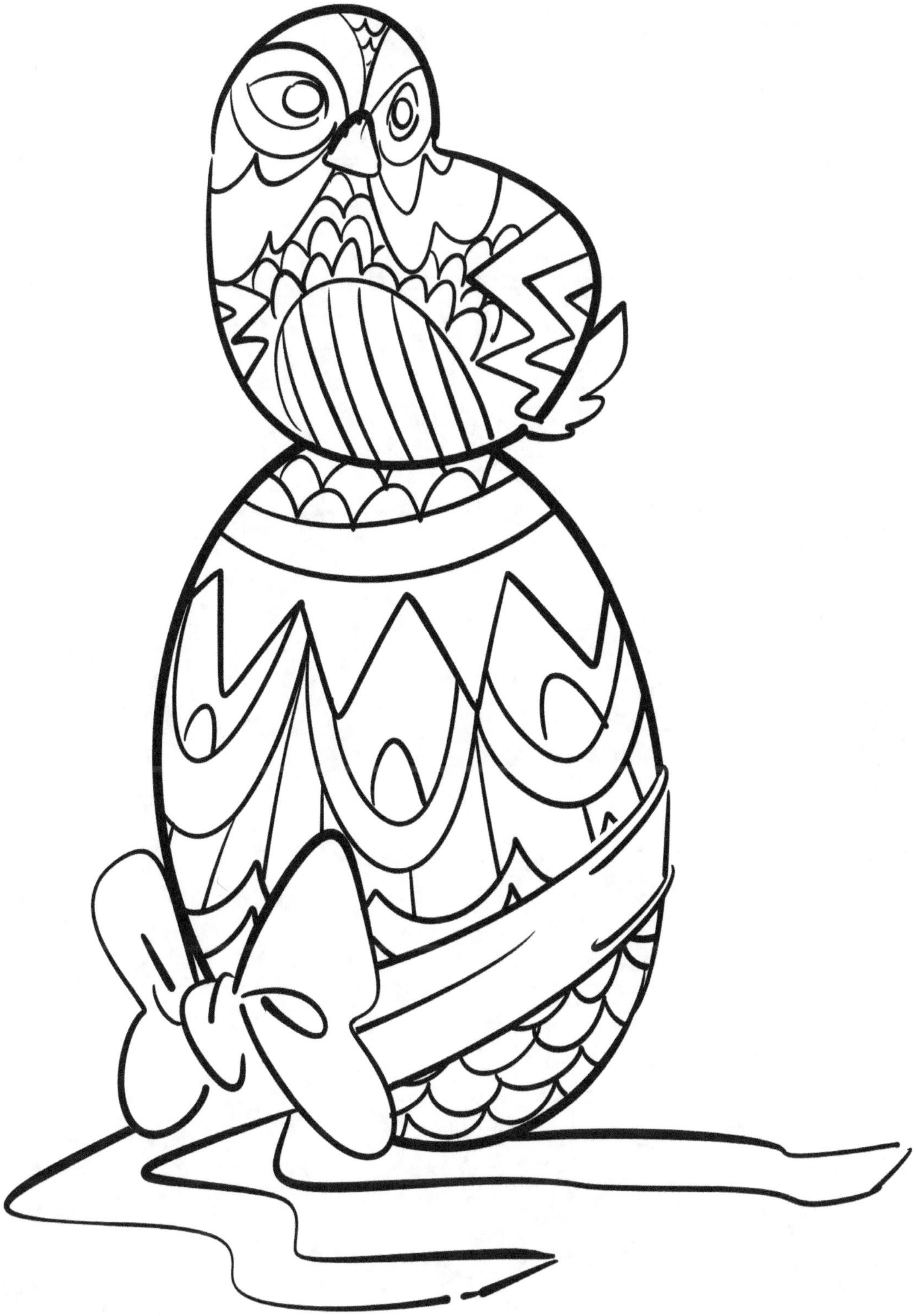

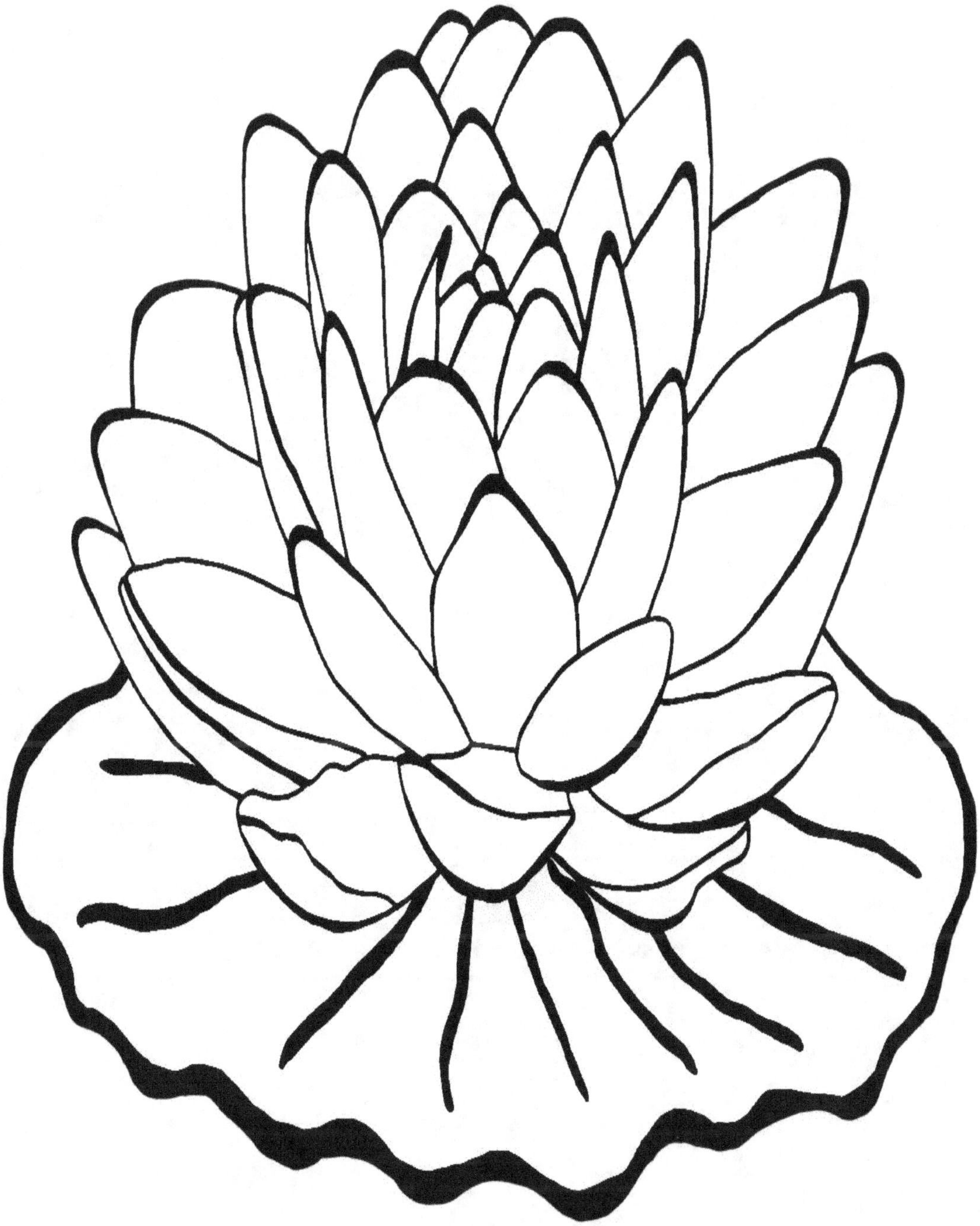

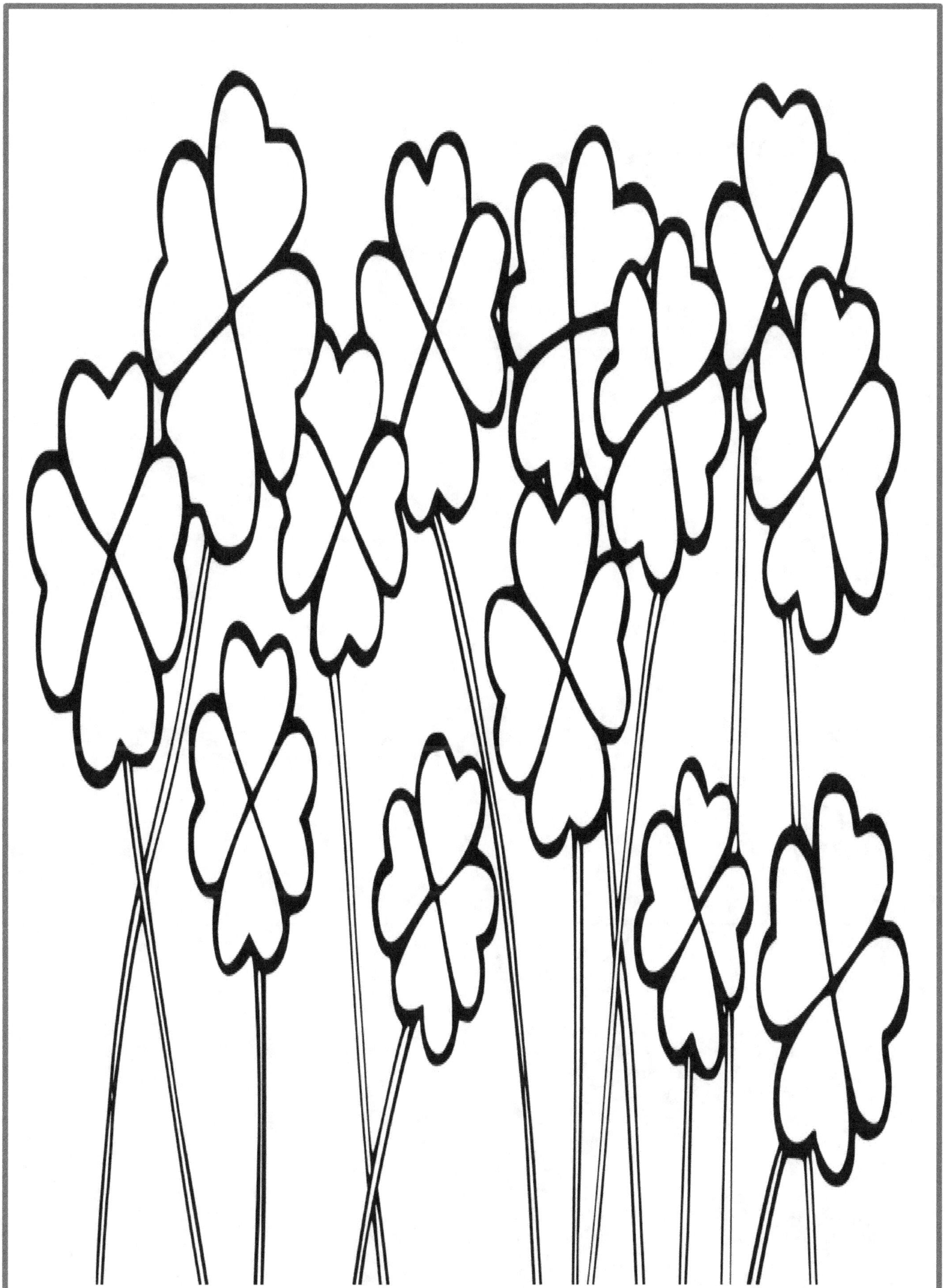

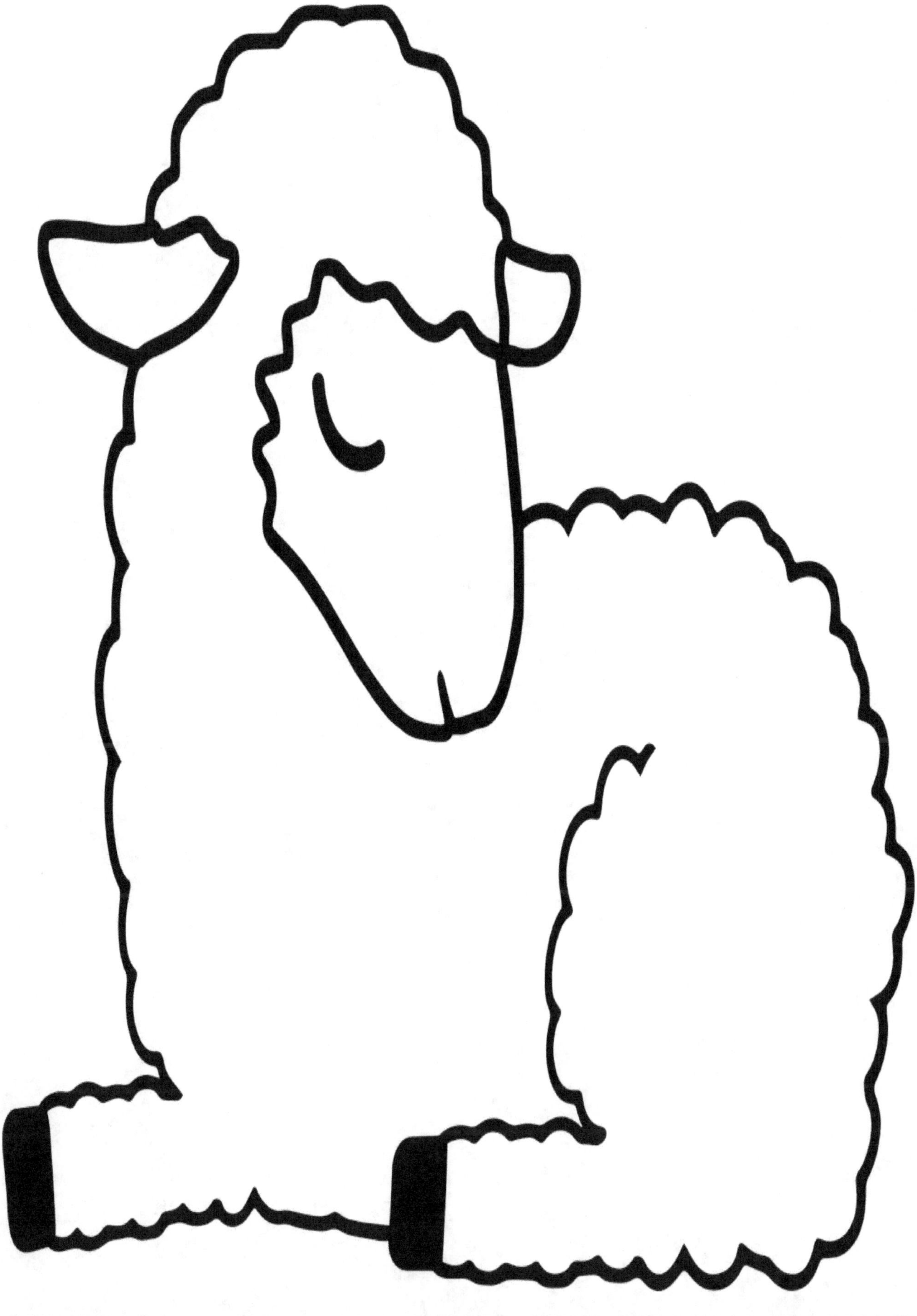

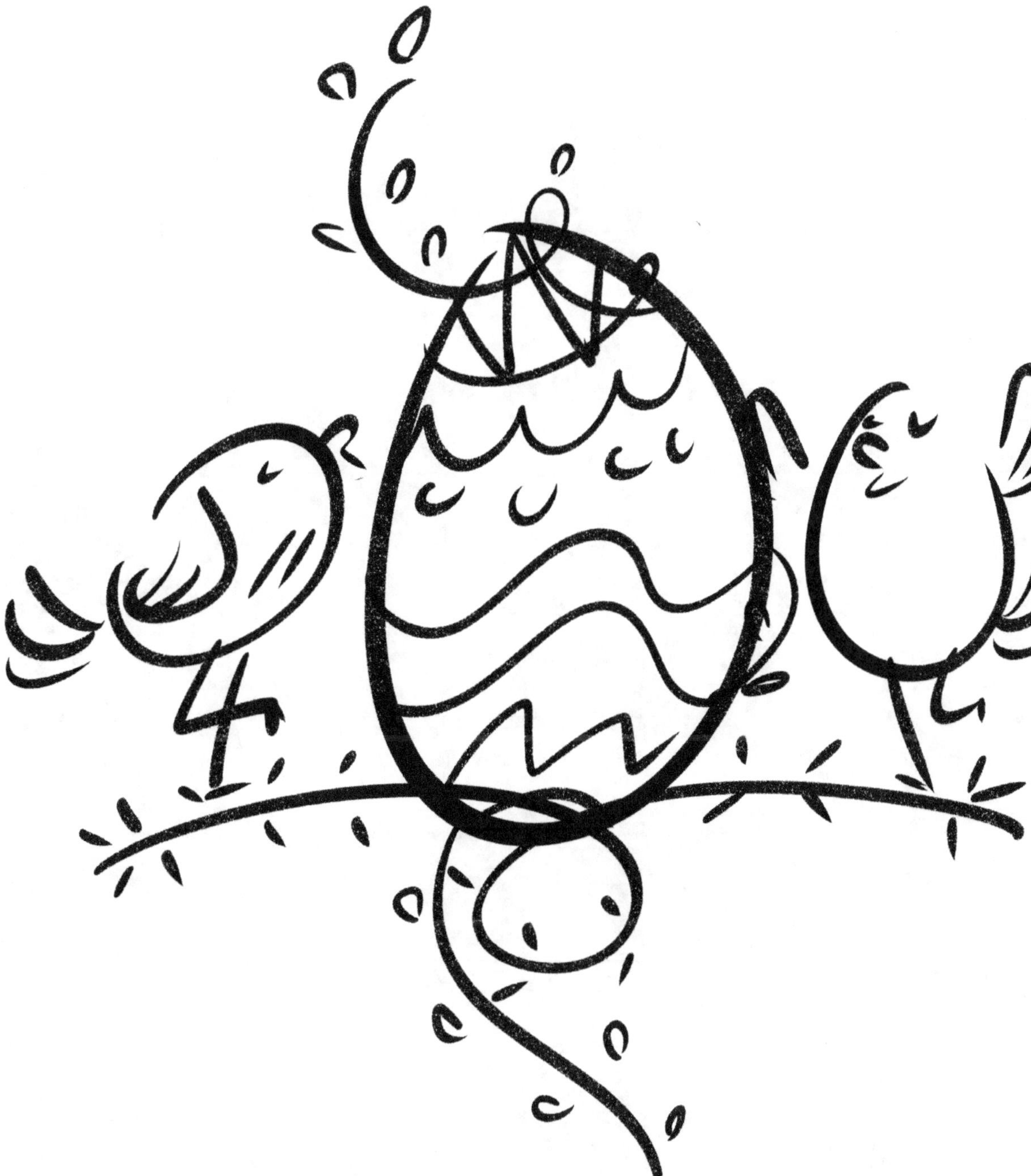

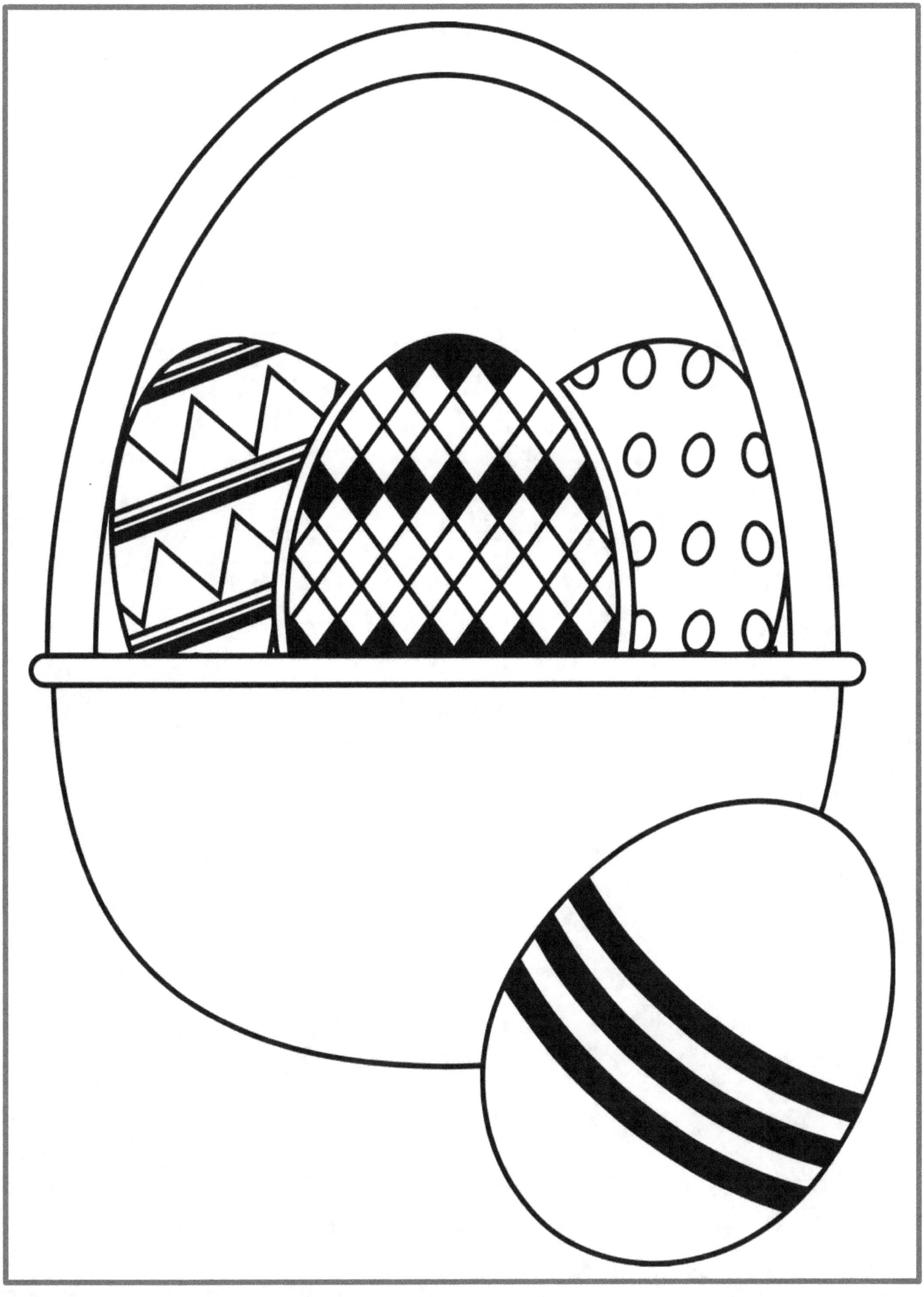

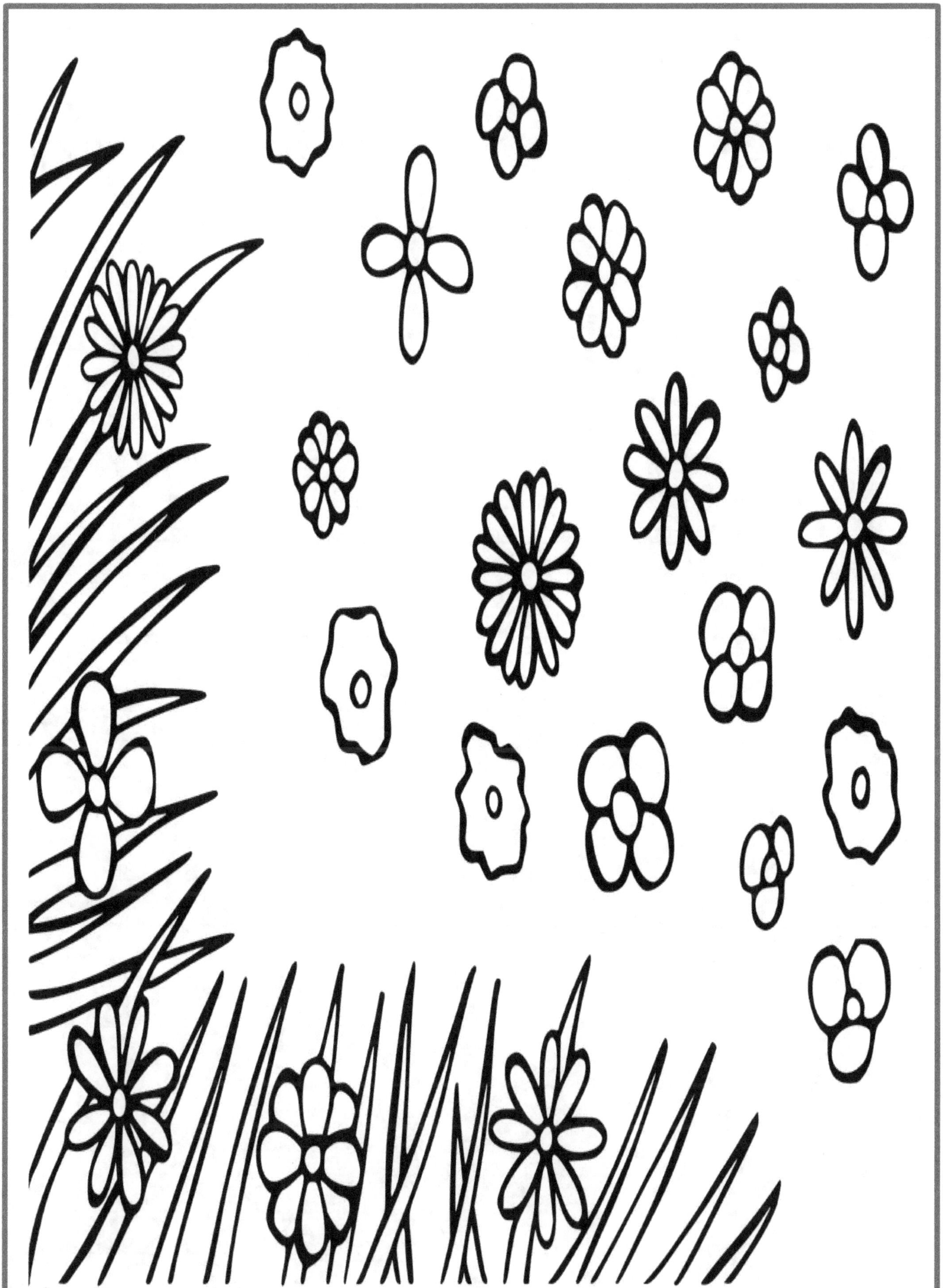

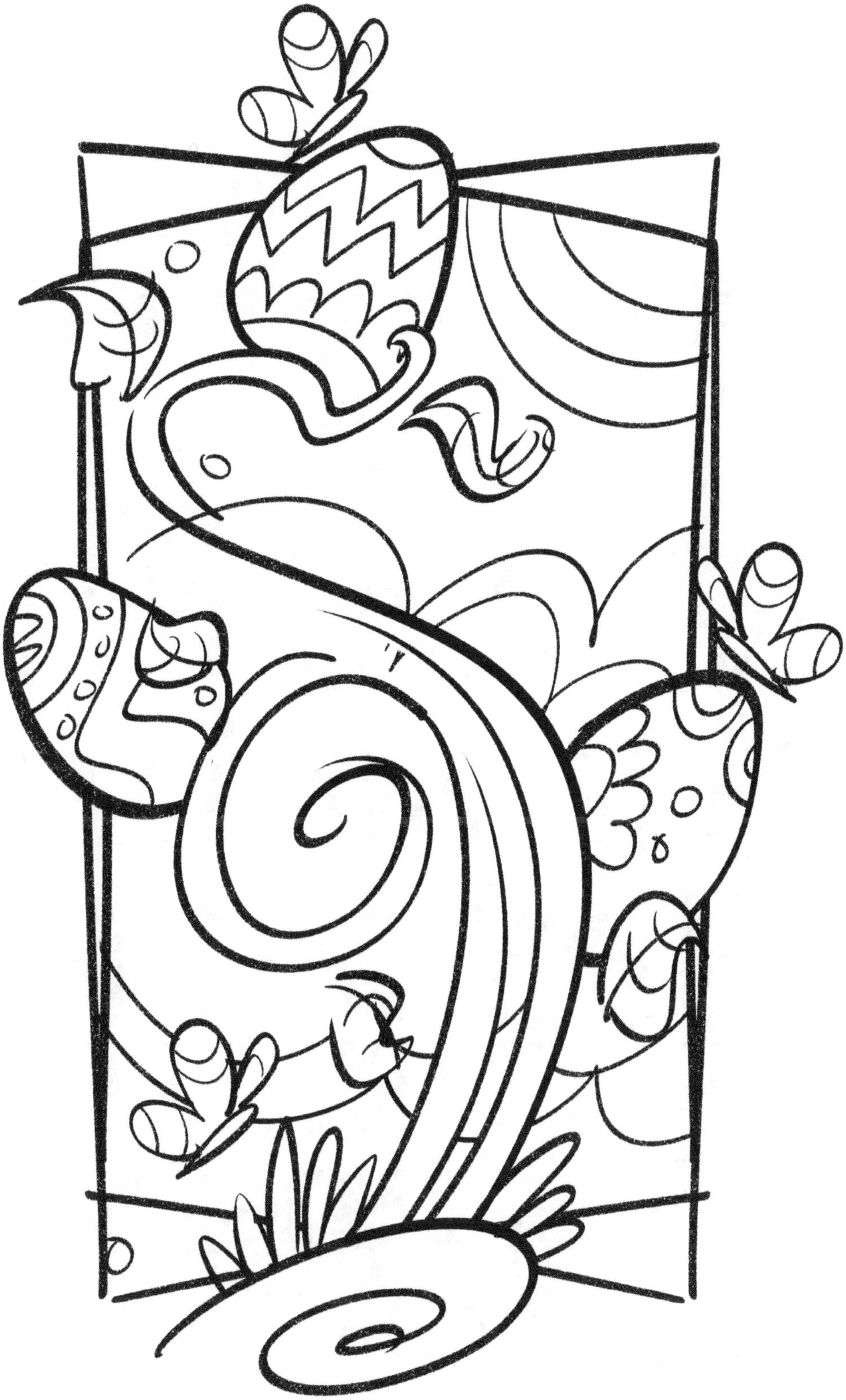

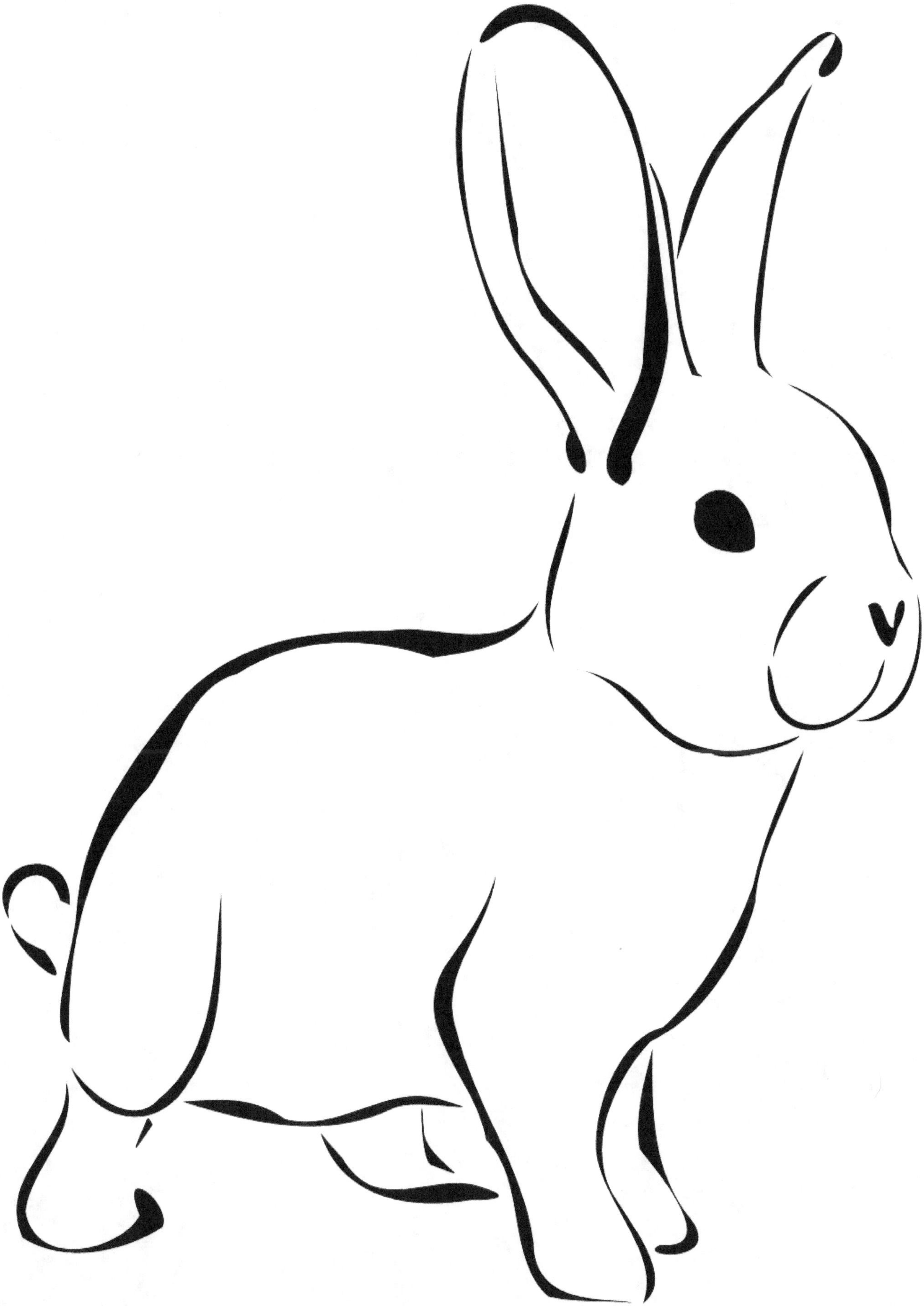

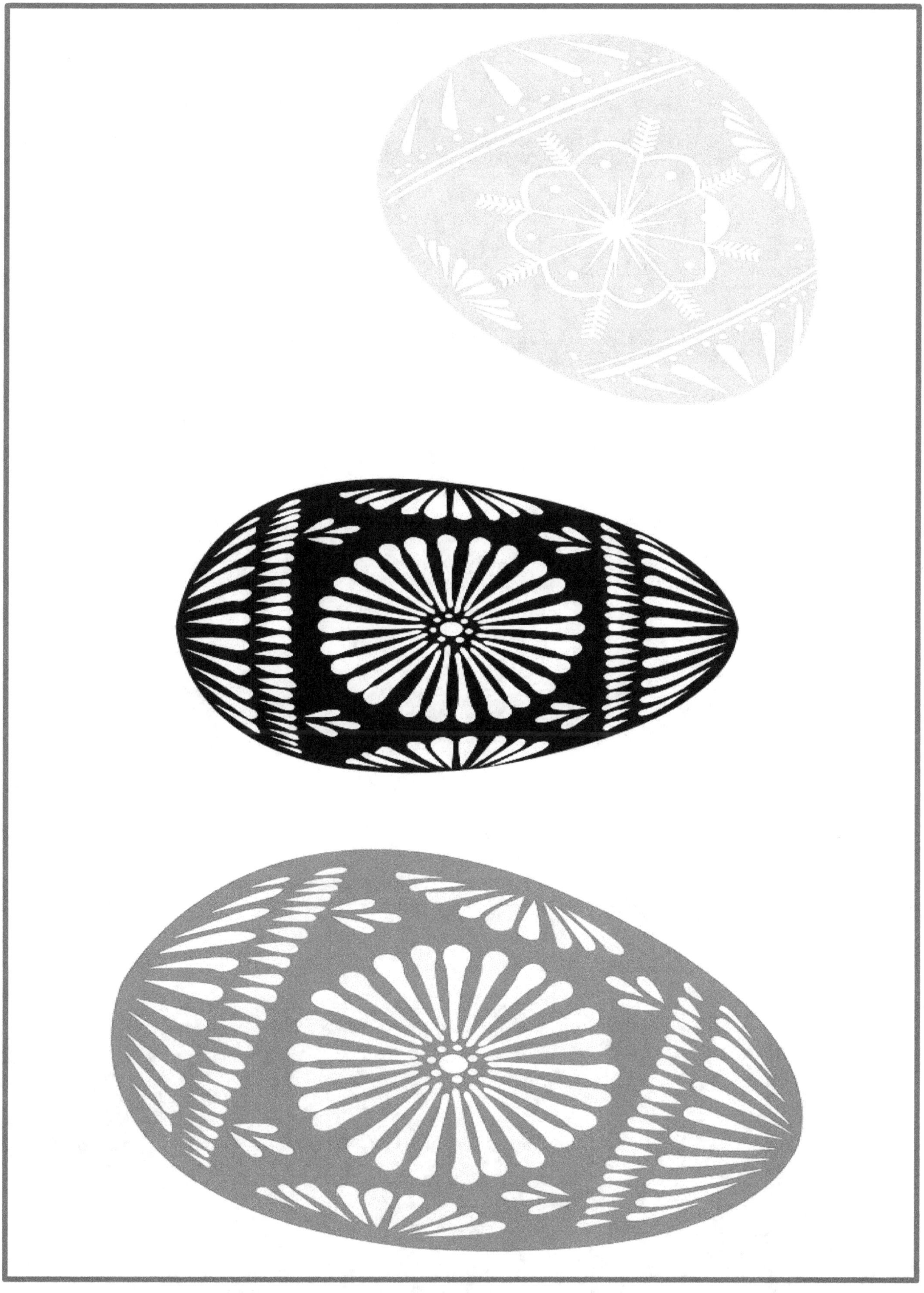

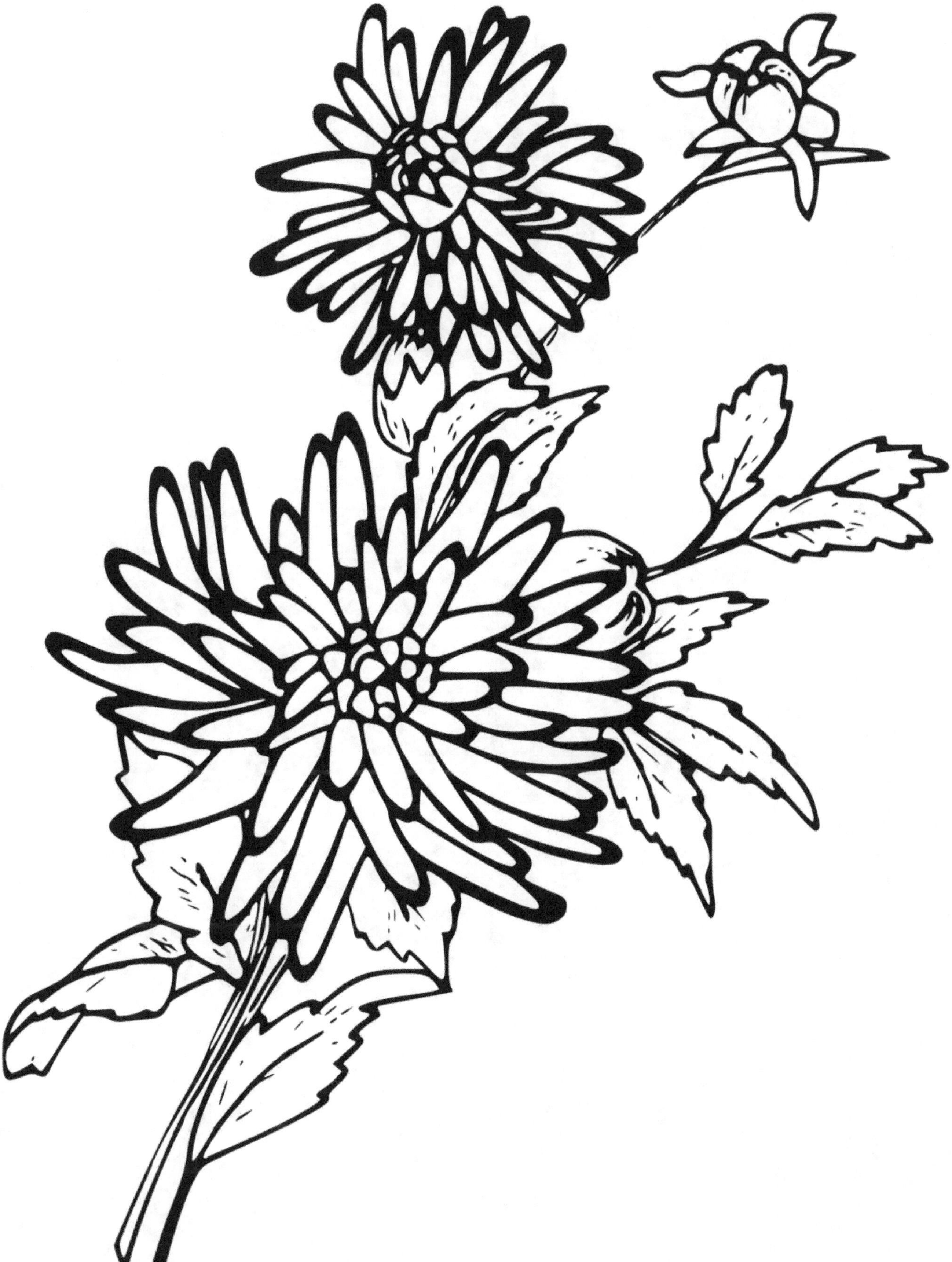

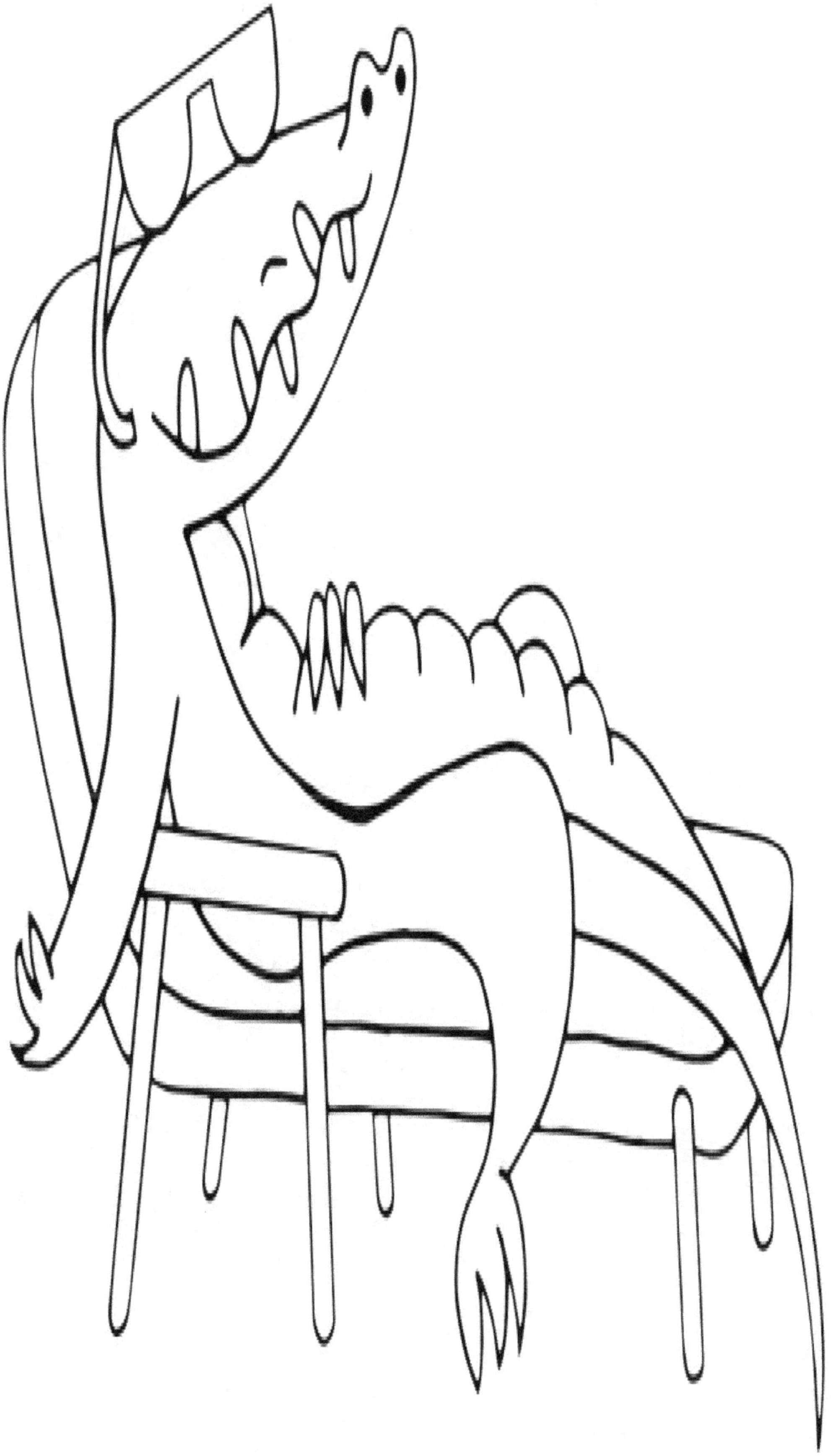

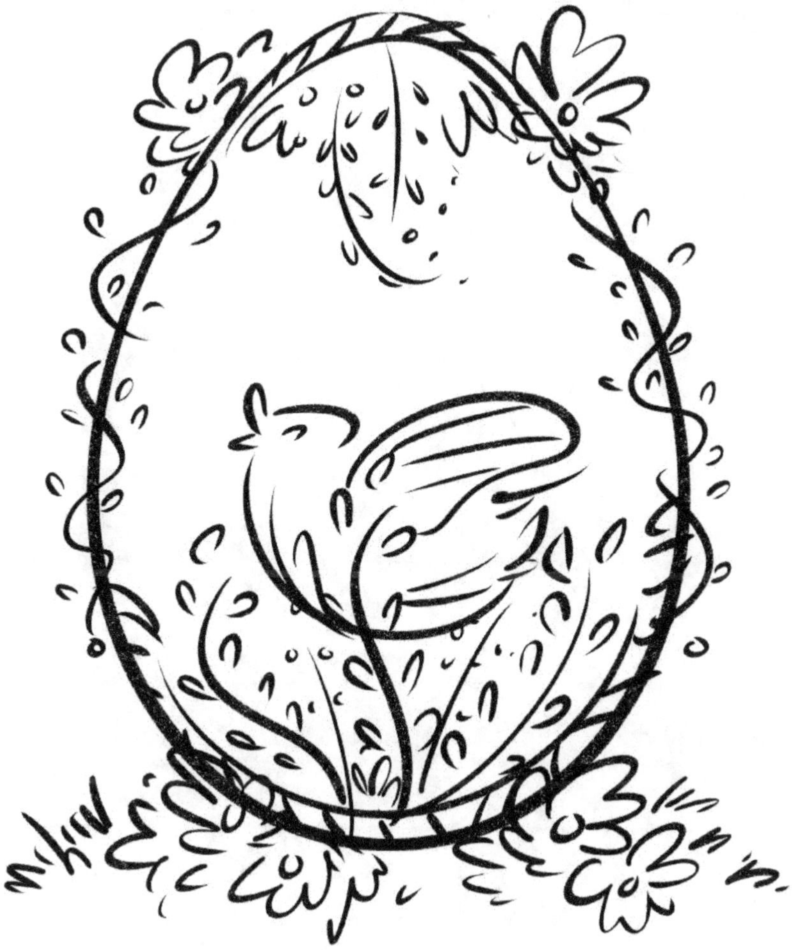

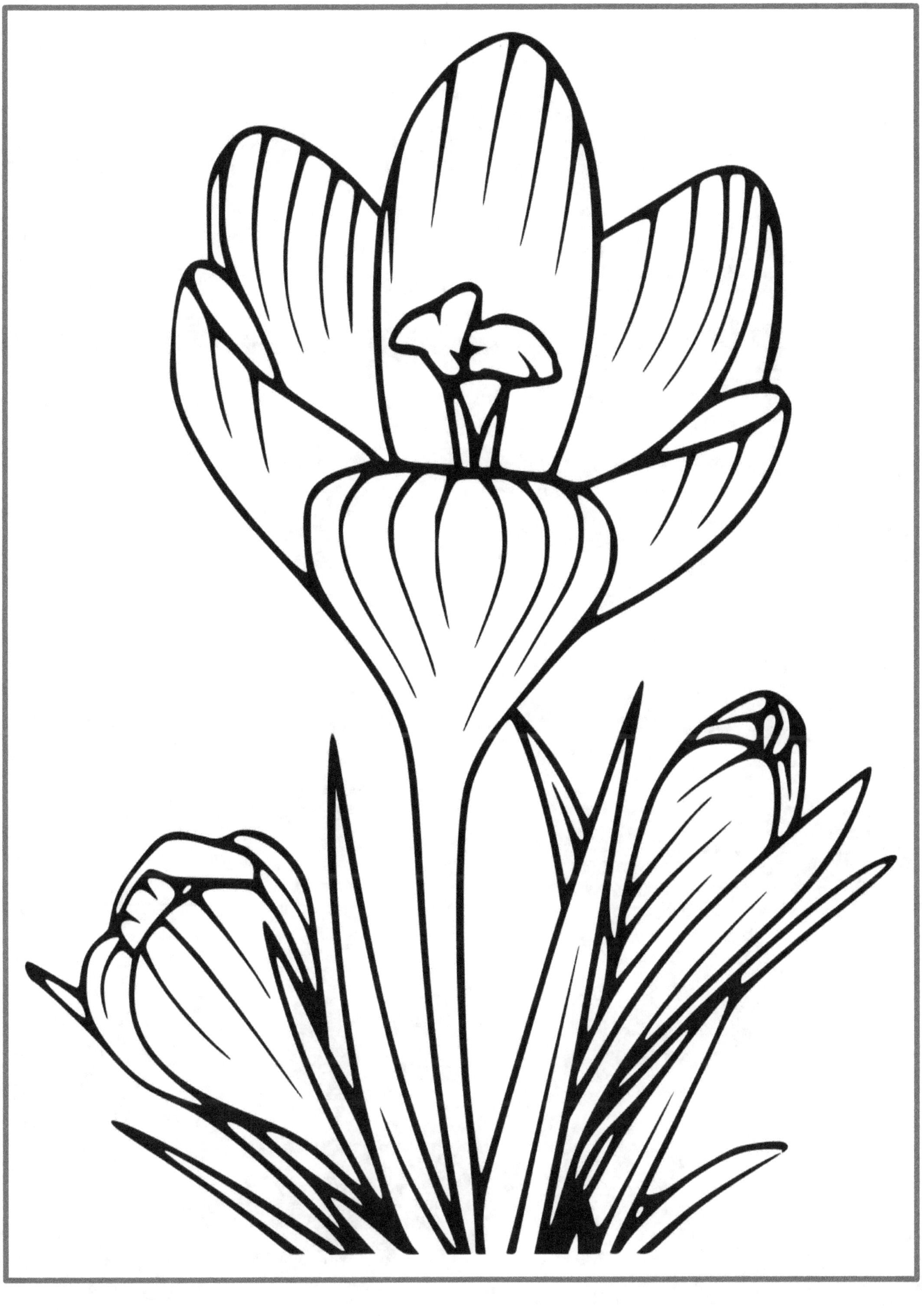

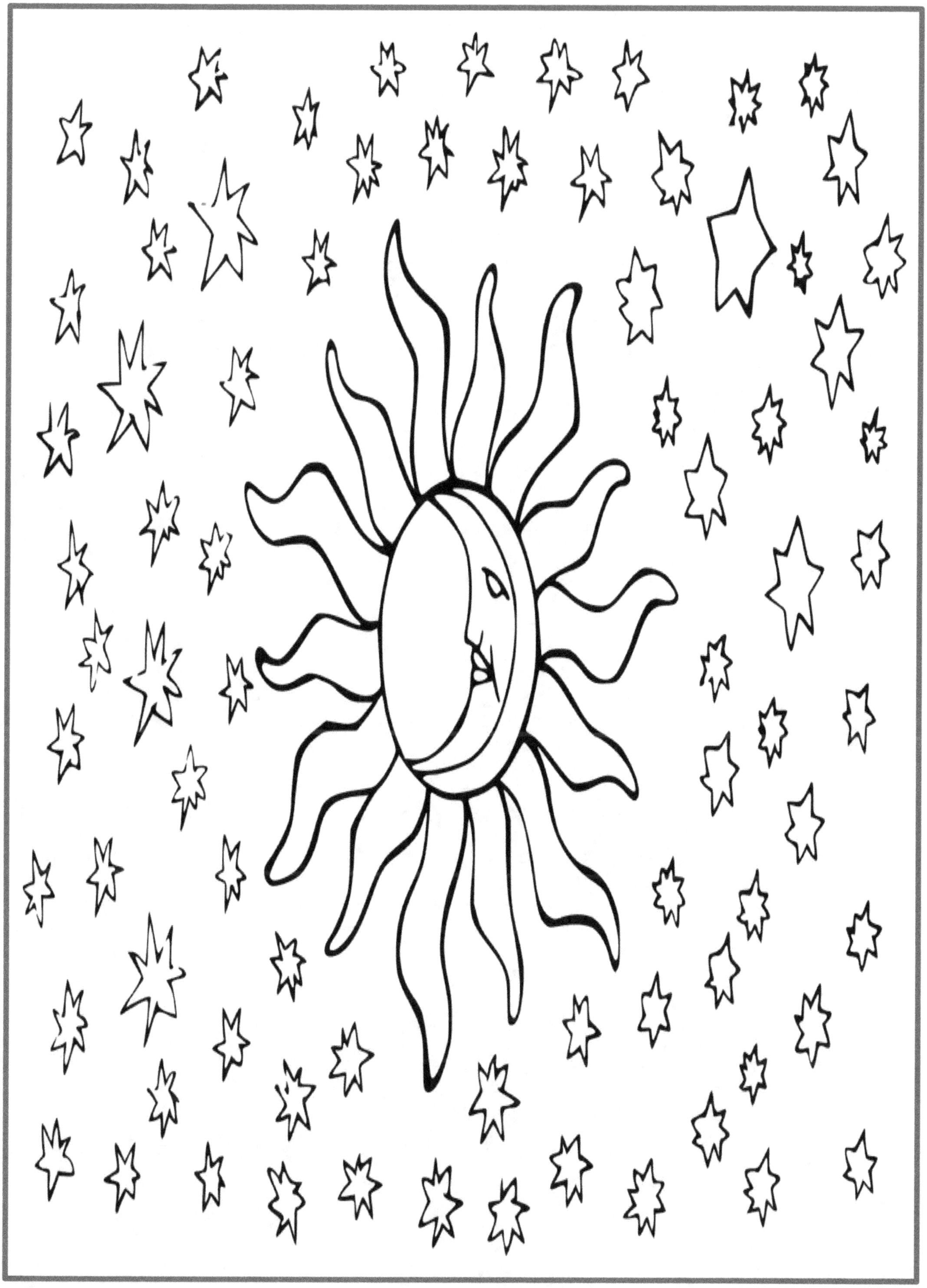

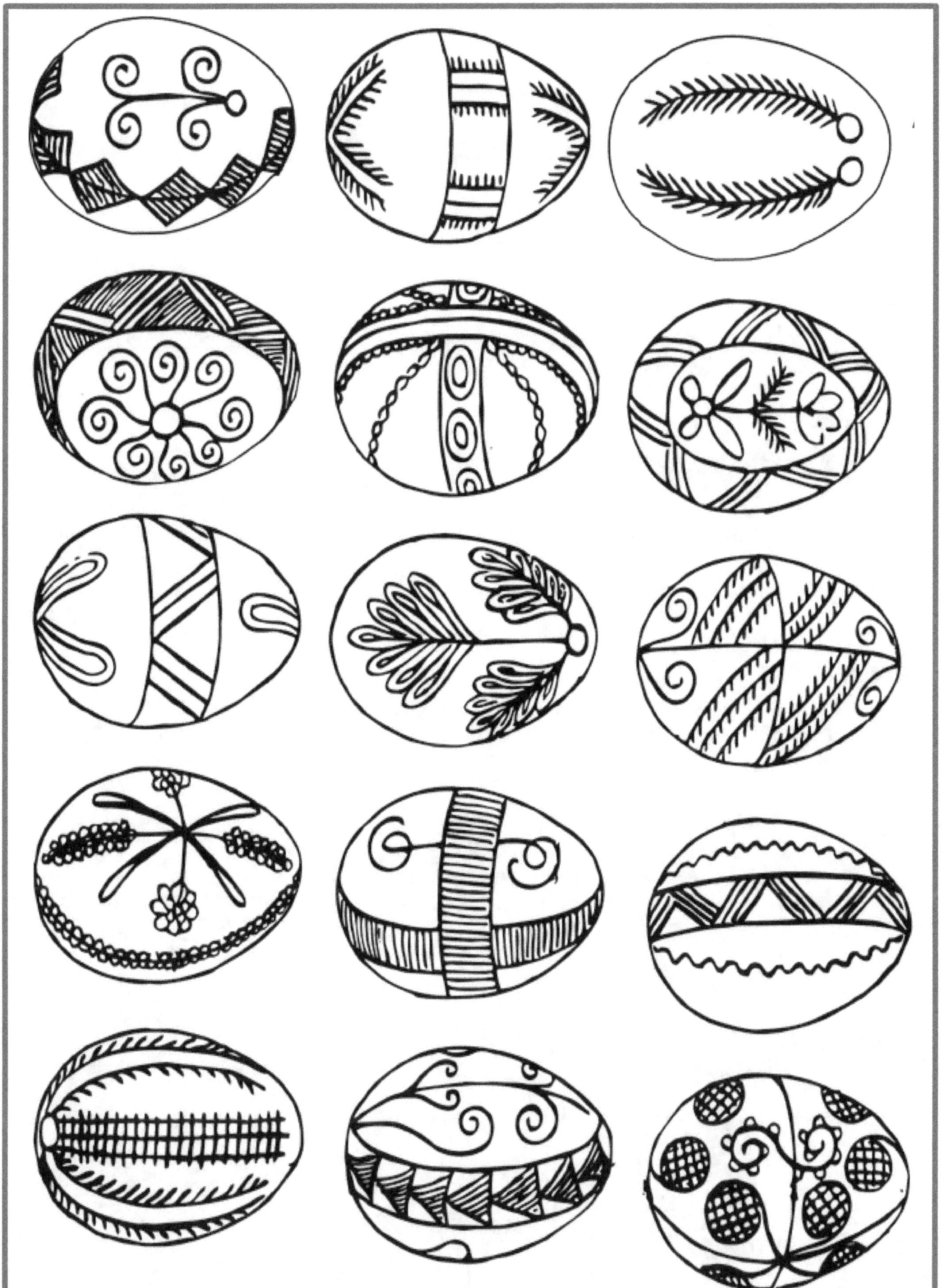

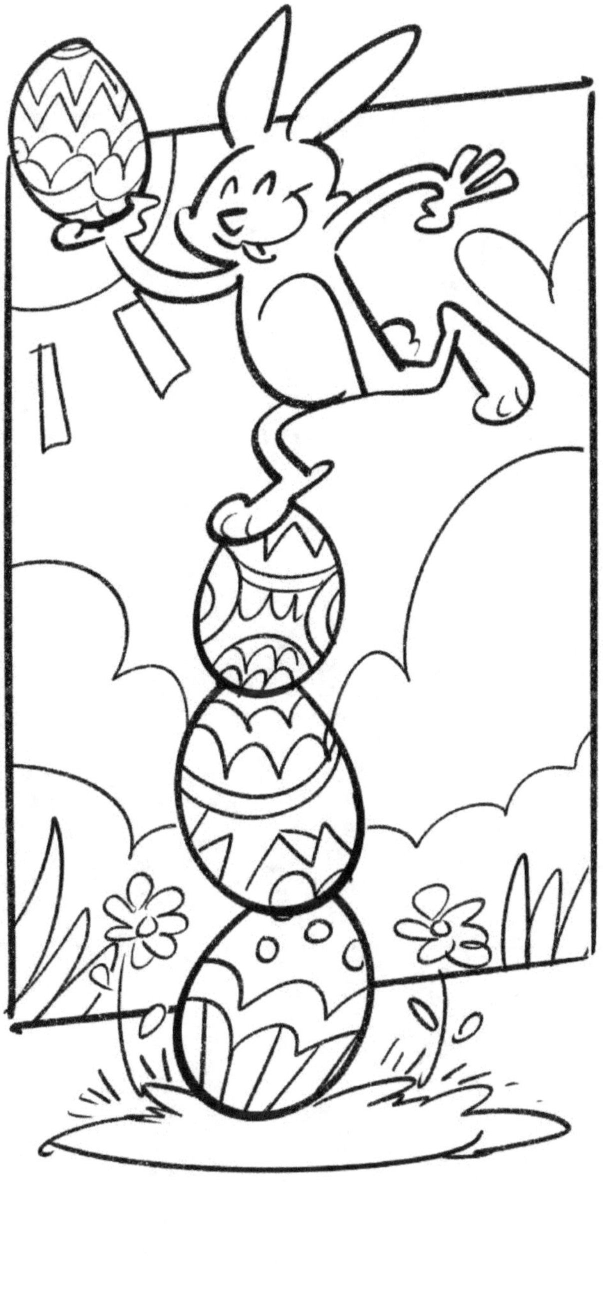

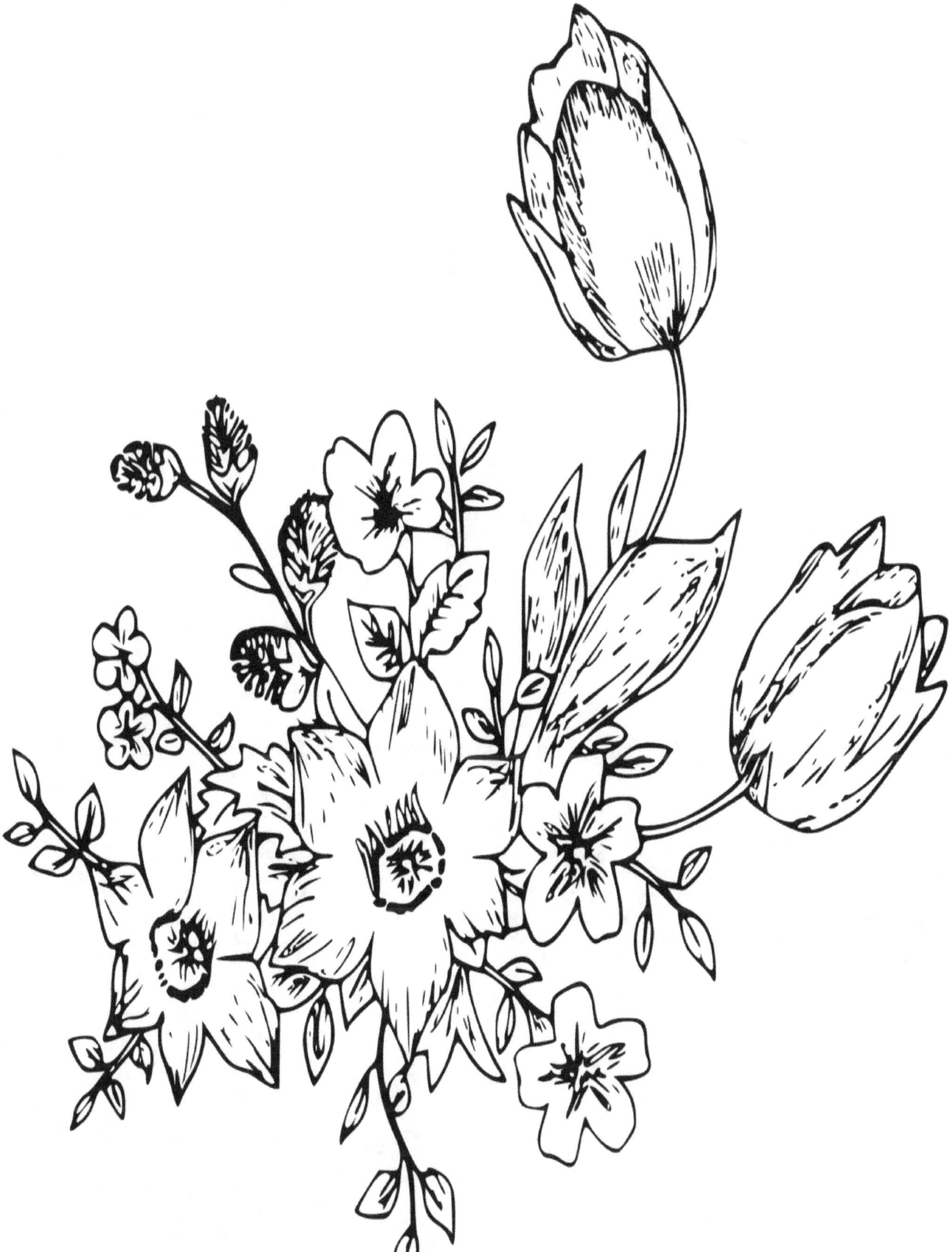

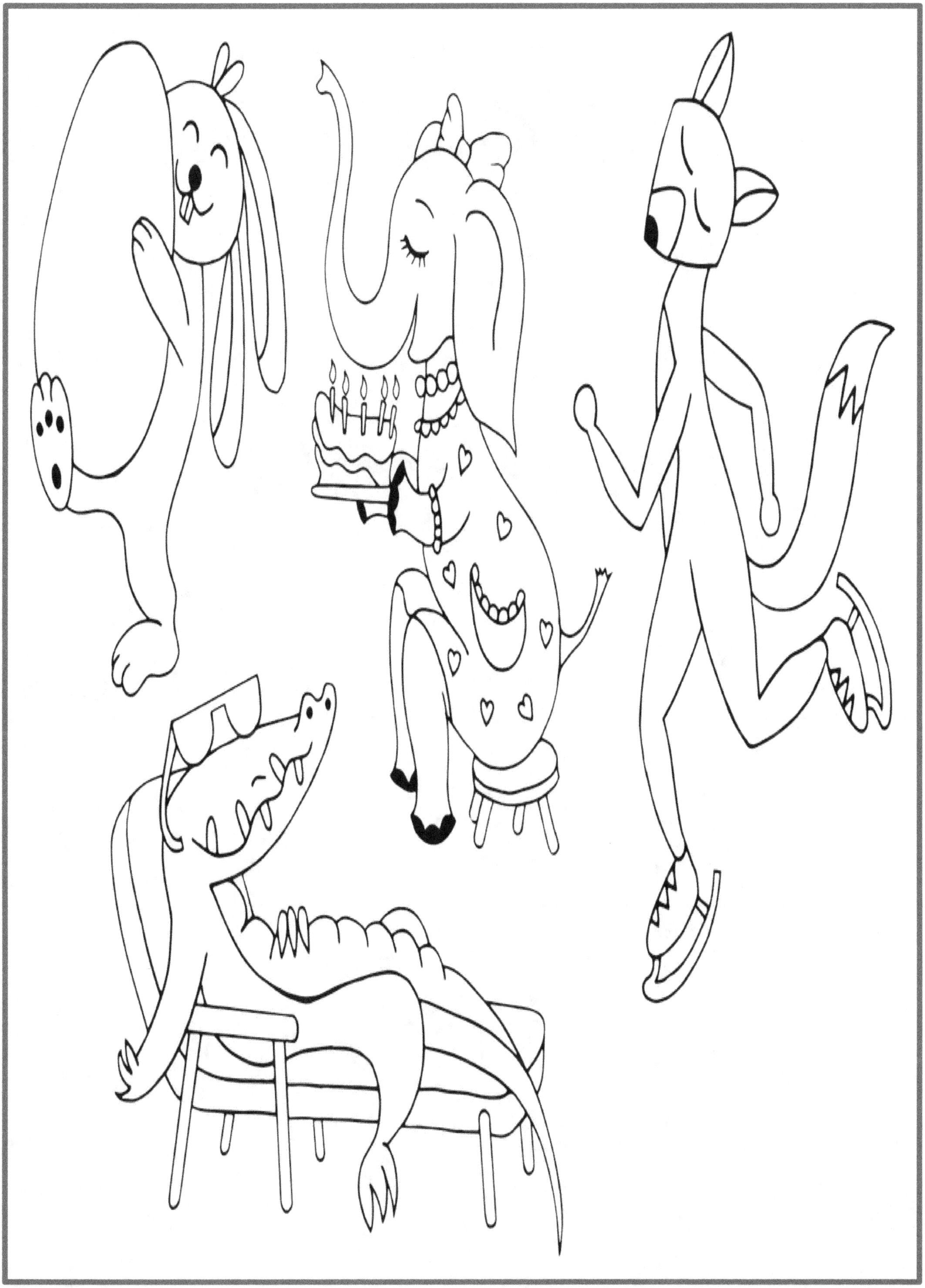

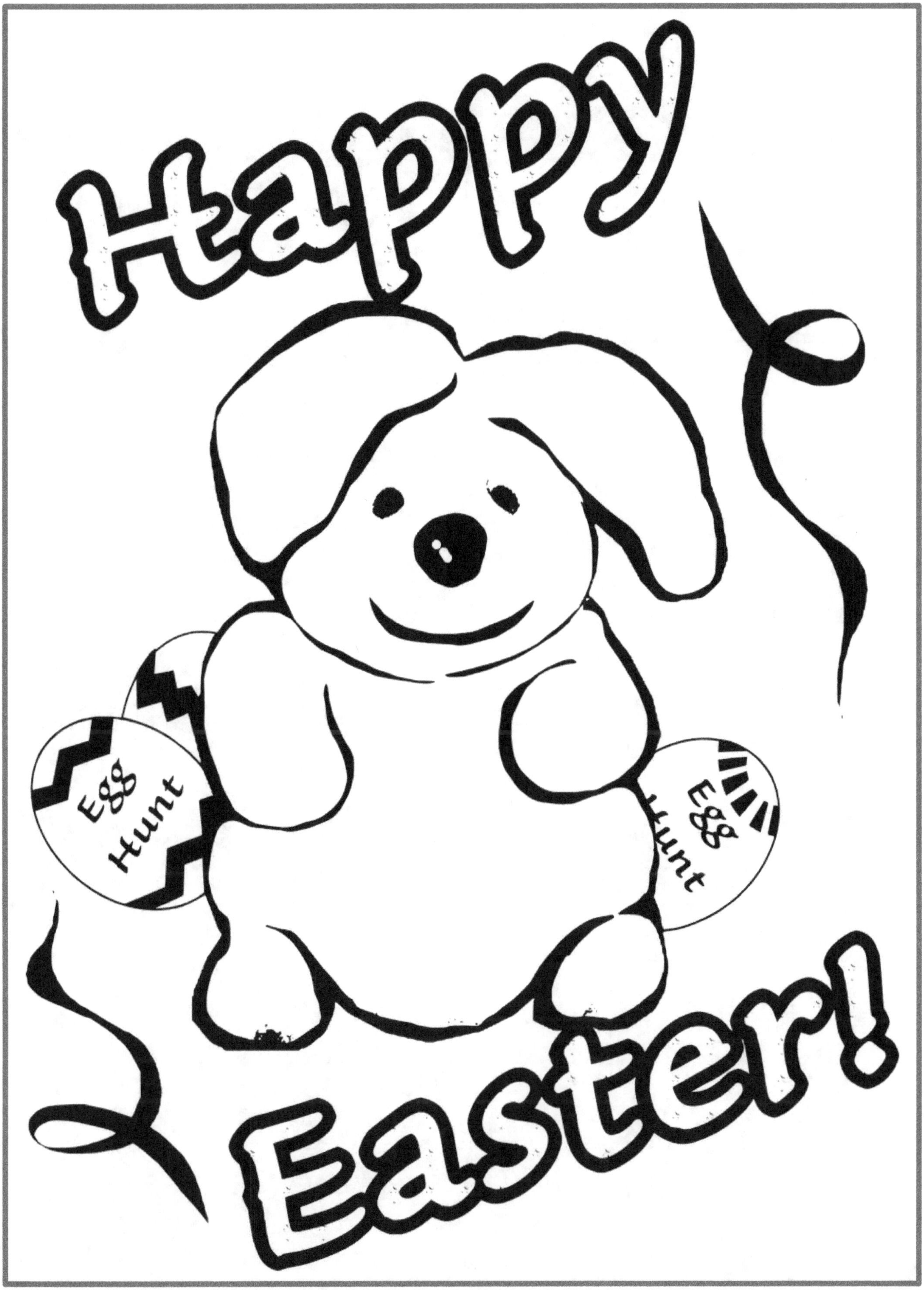
Happy
Egg Hunt
Egg Hunt
Easter!

www.ingramcontent.com/pod-product-compliance
Lightning Source LLC
Chambersburg PA
CBHW080841220526
45467CB00008B/2350
9798703315781